Meaningful Aging from a Humanist Perspective

Peter Derkx • Anthony B. Pinn

Meaningful Aging from a Humanist Perspective

palgrave
macmillan

Peter Derkx
University of Humanistic Studies
Utrecht, The Netherlands

Anthony B. Pinn
Religion Department
Rice University
Houston, TX, USA

ISBN 978-3-031-53868-1   ISBN 978-3-031-53869-8   (eBook)
https://doi.org/10.1007/978-3-031-53869-8

© The Editor(s) (if applicable) and The Author(s), under exclusive licence to Springer Nature Switzerland AG 2024
This work is subject to copyright. All rights are solely and exclusively licensed by the Publisher, whether the whole or part of the material is concerned, specifically the rights of translation, reprinting, reuse of illustrations, recitation, broadcasting, reproduction on microfilms or in any other physical way, and transmission or information storage and retrieval, electronic adaptation, computer software, or by similar or dissimilar methodology now known or hereafter developed.
The use of general descriptive names, registered names, trademarks, service marks, etc. in this publication does not imply, even in the absence of a specific statement, that such names are exempt from the relevant protective laws and regulations and therefore free for general use.
The publisher, the authors, and the editors are safe to assume that the advice and information in this book are believed to be true and accurate at the date of publication. Neither the publisher nor the authors or the editors give a warranty, expressed or implied, with respect to the material contained herein or for any errors or omissions that may have been made. The publisher remains neutral with regard to jurisdictional claims in published maps and institutional affiliations.

This Palgrave Macmillan imprint is published by the registered company Springer Nature Switzerland AG.
The registered company address is: Gewerbestrasse 11, 6330 Cham, Switzerland

Paper in this product is recyclable.

Acknowledgements

This slim volume was many years in the making. However, we want to extend our gratitude to Joachim Duyndam and Anja Machielse whose idea for a book dealing with Peter Derkx's work on the existential side of aging grounds this project. We appreciate their persistent attention to the need for this volume during the rough period of COVID up to Palgrave Macmillan contracting the project. We must also acknowledge that much of our thinking on this topic (and many others) has been made possible through the 'spaces' of exchange afforded us through the University of Humanistic Studies and the Institute for Humanist Studies, for which Pinn serves as director of research. Through programming organized and funded by these two organizations, our thinking advanced and our intellectual connection (and friendship) was forged and fueled, as we moved between Houston (TX) and Utrecht (Netherlands). And so, in a significant way, this book represents a good number of years thinking a lived humanism, a range of considered conversation partners, and institutional support.

In addition, we would like to say thank you to our editor, Philip Getz whose patience and support were invaluable, and we wish him much success as he moves into the next phase of his professional life. We must also acknowledge the work of Amy Invernizzi, who took on this project after Philip left the press. Thank you and much appreciation for the rest of the Palgrave Macmillan team for all the hard work on this volume.

Contents

1 Initial Considerations 1

2 Dimensions of Meaningful Aging 9

3 The Longevity of Justice: Assessing Peter Derkx's Approach 63

Bibliography 79

Index 91

About the Authors

Peter Derkx is emeritus professor of humanism and worldviews. He worked at the Humanist Training Institute and its successor the University of Humanistic Studies from 1977 to 2016. His teaching and research responsibilities have been in ethics, social philosophy, and the history and theory of humanism. Since 2003, he has focused on a humanist theory of meaningful aging. Three recent book chapters: *The Future of Humanism* (2015), *A Humanist Evaluation of Substantial Life Extension Through Biomedical Research and Technology* (2016), and (with Hanne Laceulle) *Humanism and Aging* (2021).

Anthony B. Pinn is currently the Agnes Cullen Arnold Distinguished Professor of Humanities and professor of religion at Rice University. Pinn is a fellow of the American Academy of Arts and Sciences, and he is a Professor Extraordinarius at the University of South Africa. Pinn is the founding director of the Center for Engaged Research and Collaborative Learning at Rice University. In addition, he is Director of Research for the Institute for Humanist Studies—a Washington, DC-based think tank. Pinn's research interests include religion and culture; black religious thought; humanism; and, hip hop culture. He is the author/editor of over 35 books, including *The Oxford Handbook of Humanism* (2021) and the novel, *The New Disciples* (2015).

CHAPTER 1

Initial Considerations

Abstract This chapter offers context for the volume by situating the two essays that anchor this slim book. It highlights the manner in which COVID amplified a concern with death and the challenges of living well in a context of uncertain safeguards for health. What does it mean to live well in a context of such profound disruption and demise? For those who are theists, such misery is addressed through theological claims that use faith as a guiding force in the face of existential crisis. Yet, what of those who are non-theists, who are humanists? In this context, the question of living well, of productive aging, raised by Peter Derkx gains an amplified significance. It is in response to this question that Peter's framing of a meaningful life as connected to a productive process of change over time— i.e., aging—offered in his essay marks a significant contribution to humanism. Pinn's essay seeks to account for Derkx's contributions while raising questions concerning the cultural context for aging and assumptions concerning what it means to age well within our social world.

Keywords Well-being · Meaningful life · Aging · Human · Humanism · COVID-19 · Death

This slim volume started as an edited text by Joachim Duyndam and Anja Machielse meant to situate and explore Peter Derkx's significant intervention regarding a humanist concept of living well. Over time, and based on a good number of conversations, an adequate study of Derkx's scholarship was understood to require two volumes. This, the first of the two, includes an extended essay by Derkx and my critical response. The second, written for the most part by scholars in his subfield, is a collection that seeks to extend his intellectual endeavors. The overall project first started some years ago with an in-person meeting at the University of Humanistic Studies (in the Netherlands), but things would change radically before all the work was done.

COVID-19 not only altered development of this project; it also amplified the importance of such attention to well-being. Across the globe, death came through the most modest of contacts—sharing space in which the virus moved unseen due to a laugh, a hug, a cough. The closeness we crave, the pleasure of togetherness, was marked by a danger—the potential that proximity would result in painful loss. The stability of human life, while never an equitable circumstance, deteriorated further. In other words, as was stated in 2020:

> The COVID-19 pandemic has led to a dramatic loss of human life worldwide and presents an unprecedented challenge to public health, food systems and the world of work. The economic and social disruption caused by the pandemic is devastating: tens of millions of people are at risk of falling into extreme poverty, while the number of undernourished people, currently estimated at nearly 690 million, could increase by up to 132 million by the end of the year.[1]

COVID-19 is one of the more recent examples of how the nature and meaning of life is a vulnerable and fragile arrangement. This health crisis wasn't simply a medical concern. No, for those who were attuned to the undertones of conversation and media reports, deep existential considerations surfaced with force and demanded attention. One need only think about the ways in which COVID-19 amplified and warped issues of theodicy, for instance—i.e., what can one say about God in light of such

---

[1] "Impact of COVID-19 on people's livelihoods, their health and our food systems," Joint statement by ILO, FAO, IFAD and WHO, October 13, 2020. Found at: https://www.who.int/news/item/13-10-2020-impact-of-covid-19-on-people's-livelihoods-their-health-and-our-food-systems

massive death that took the young and innocent? Or, raised questions concerning the nature and meaning of humanity—and the human's relationship to the larger arrangement of life. As a consequence, and in response to such pressing theological questions, there were ways in which COVID-19 served to exaggerate some moral and ethical intents and claims from theistic traditions meant to provide methods of addressing a basic desire for meaning and for a happy life. For example, for some Christians COVID-19 became something of a moral lesson that pointed out the need for adherence to and faith in the metaphysical decrees of their tradition. Such religious commitment might not prevent physical death, but it would position them, despite demise, for life *after* death—a refined existence free of the traumas and shortcomings that mark this current existence. I would venture to say, the ability to provide assurances with respect to death and dying is one of the significant appeals of religious commitment for many—the underlying rationale for adherence to the 'faith'—particularly in the type of angst generating context produced by COVID-19.

But the significant growth in the percentage of 'nones' in some countries and the long tradition of skepticism and freethought in others, urge a question: What of those who live outside the working of theistic traditions but also faced the dead-dealing challenge of COVID-19 and other traumas? While there are assurances offered within various forms of theism, what is available to those who are non-believers? For example, how should humanists understand death and dying in this particular historical moment? Or, better yet, what are the markers of a happy life when the will of God(s) and the influence of other cosmic forces are removed from consideration?

If there's nothing after this life, it only follows that for humanists the goal is to maximize the value of this movement through the material world. Without any concern for what is next, a humanist would be motivated to make the most of this time, to maximize all that generates responsible happiness as an individual and as a member of a larger (perhaps global) community within the confines of human history. Related to this framing of basic concern, there is the accompanying question of what it actually means to live well over time. In a word, what constitutes a meaningful life? And, what practices and patterns of interaction support the effort to achieve a meaningful life? What might hamper one's ability to live well as a humanist? How does one even go about measuring and working toward life as meaningful? Mindful of such questions and in light of the fact that humanists claim no adherence to a sense of something beyond this physical existence, humanism is marked—at least implicitly—by a keen and consistent attention to living within the context of our materiality. As Sarah Bakewell's *Humanly Possible: Seven Hundred Years of Humanist Freethinking, Inquiry, and Hope* points out, much humanist attention over the centuries has been given to questions and concerns related to living well—to generating as much fulfillment as possible. This wrestling with the elements of a happy life is a matter of orientation and of one's posture toward the predicaments and possibilities lodged within encounters in and with the world. And something of this sentiment is found in Bakewell's statement near the end of the introduction to *Humanly Possible*. She writes, when reflecting on tension between and structures of anti-humanist and humanist sensibilities:

> Anti-humanism usefully reminds us not to be vain or complacent; it supplies a bracing realism about what is weak or nefarious in us. It reminds us not to be naïve, and prepares us for the fact that, at any moment, we and our fellows are likely to do something stupid or wicked. It forces humanism to keep working to justify itself. Meanwhile, humanism warns us against neglecting the tasks of our current world in favor of dreams of paradise, whether on this earth or elsewhere. It helps to counter the intoxicating promises of extremists, and it wards off the despair that can come from obsessing too much over our faults. Instead of a defeatism that blames all problems on God, or our own biology, or historical inevitability, it reminds us of our human responsibility for what we do with our lives and urges us to keep our attention on earthly challenges and on our shared well-being.[2]

Whether through various traditions of education, or framings of community and practices of interaction, or structures of political and cultural engagement, humanists have explored ways to make the most of life.

A host of others have shared such a line of reasoning, a framing of humanism's obligations and intent with respect to well-being. Alice Roberts and Andrew Copson's *The Little Book of Humanism: Universal Lessons on Finding Purpose, Meaning, and Joy*, for instance, presents another example of humanist attention to the framework for and practices

---

[2] Sarah Bakewell (2023) *Humanly Possible: Seven Hundred Years of Humanist Freethinking, Inquiry, and Hope* New York: Penguin Press, pp. 21–22.

related to well-being.[3] Such themes also undergird Greg Epstein's *Good Without God: What a Billion Nonreligious People Do Believe*, a book which captures a positive framing of humanism geared toward its thought and practice derived in such a way as to allow humanism to replace the work generally associated with (theistic) religion.[4] And in offering this apology for humanism, one cannot help but recognize that Epstein is really getting at what humanists understand as the value of life and how one goes about arranging one's praxis so as to maximize human potential. This, I would suggest, is another way of talking about meaningful living. Finally, for humanist activists such as Candace Gorham, living in a meaningful manner has to involve keen attention to mental health and related issues that might hamper well-being, particularly for humanists coming from (and living within) marginalized communities.[5]

My aim here isn't to provide a rehearsal of humanist literature on well-being and living well. Instead, I mention the above texts simply to offer a few examples of what constitutes a rich area of study for humanists from various backgrounds, professions, and communities. Both academic and popular work related to living well are informed by an important contextual fact: Meaningful life is an arranged consideration, which is to say it marks out a geography of time and space occupied in ways that generate certain physical and psychological results—and the body shifts and changes during this process. *In other words, a meaningful life has to account for the process of aging.* There are stages of well-being that reflect the changes to our physical bodies and psychological constitution. And so, in relationship to the question of a meaningful life, there is the comparable and related question of aging well—or, meaningful aging. That is to say, attention to what it means to live has to recognize and respond to the embodied changes that take place within the context of the body over time. Between birth and death is aging.

Peter Derkx, emeritus Professor of Humanism and Worldviews at the University of Humanistic Studies, has spent his career forging an impressive reputation for scholarship at the intersection of meaningful living and aging well—explored through the conceptual framework of humanism as

---
[3] Alice Roberts and Andrew Copson (2022) *The Little Book of Humanism: Universal Lessons on Finding Purpose, Meaning, and Joy*. London: Piatkus.
[4] Greg Epstein (2009) *Good Without God: What a Billion Nonreligious People Do Believe*. New York: Harper Collins.
[5] Candace Gorham (2021) *On Death, Dying, and Disbelief*. Durham, NC: Pitchstone Publishing.

a socio-cultural orientation, or what Derkx labels a "worldview." For Derkx, humanism as a source of orientation has to entail attention to what it means to be human in ways that are existentially engaged and historically mindful. And so, humanism has an opportunity (if not obligation) to offer a creative and compelling intervention into the joys and challenges associated with the aging body and mind—making of significant concern what it means to live meaningfully in a body that is slowing (but not always slowly) decaying; or, perhaps a gentler way to frame it is to say the body slowly succumbs to reduced function and lowered vitality.

Much celebrated humanist thought is marked by a radical optimism that seems to assume a static depiction of the human—lodged in a body resistant to the worse aspects of material circumstances and supple enough to thrive despite all. Now, some might claim I'm overstating the case, and this might be. However, what Derkx's scholarship suggests on some level is recognition that the humanist body is vulnerable, 'porous' in numerous ways, and subject to more than its will in that it is a materiality that suffers the effects of decline. According to Derkx a rational, scientific, exploration of aging provides humanism with an important dimension of its humanizing effect by highlighting the changes over time to the human within *human*ism. I've followed his thinking on such issues for some time now.

Over more than a dozen years, Derkx and I have worked together, engaged in a variety of topics and concerns—primarily through his involvement with the Institute for Humanist Studies for which I have served as director of research. Our collaboration took me to Utrecht on more than a few occasions and Derkx to Houston (Texas) as well. Yet, our overlapping concerns had not, until now, produced opportunity for exchange on the issue of aging well. He'd written pieces on this topic for several of my publications; but my response hadn't gone beyond editorial feedback before I submitted those books to the various publishers. This slim volume involves a change by offering direct engagement.

Here, Derkx frames his thinking on aging well as it has developed over several decades, and I provide critical reflection on his work. And I do so with a clear motivation to explore how his theorization holds when issues of difference—e.g., race and class—are considered and are figured into the challenges of aging within the 'West,' with forms of injustice built into this social world. How does one live well within a context of discrimination? How does one age well and how is aging well measured in a context in which marginalized communities experience increased risk and reduced resource? How does one negotiate both the promise of a fruitful existence undergirding the optimism of humanism *and* attention to the limitations of that vision of life by means of which social markers—like race—can result in death due to stigmatization? How should humanists championing meaningful aging respond to recent tragedies, such as those highlighted by the protests of Black Lives Matter across the globe? Or, the traumas experienced by migrants seeking positive prospects of aging within what they perceive to be more hospitable geographies—only to be met with ongoing displacement and the threat of death without dignity?

Such questions and considerations as those above ground my response to Derkx's approach to aging. Differences between the two of us will be obvious to readers. Still, each in his own way, and in relationship to our particular sensitivities and emphases, believes forging strategies for a meaningful life requires attention to a vision of aging cognizant of the social worlds that impinge upon populations. What is the value of a humanist vision that doesn't recognize and seek to address both the promise and pitfalls of embodied life transitions? With that said, we leave it to readers to determine their own perspectives on a humanist vision for aging as a meaningful and fulfilling process. Agree or disagree with either one of us (or both of us), but engage the text nonetheless because there are ways in which our collective well-being demands attention to the range of questions and issues highlighted in these pages.

CHAPTER 2

Dimensions of Meaningful Aging

Abstract Starting from Roy Baumeister's theory, the present author has developed a theory of a meaningful life involving seven needs for meaning: needs for purpose, moral worth, self-worth, control, coherence, connectedness, and excitement. More than Baumeister's theory this one strikes a balance between agency and communion. After outlining the theory, the seven meaning dimensions are elaborated on in relation to aging. Concepts are clarified, results of (mostly recent) empirical research are reviewed, and many questions will be raised. The relation between the seven components and the relation between meaning and well-being is discussed. Finally, a plea is made for interdisciplinary collaboration between social sciences, history, and philosophy (especially ethics and social philosophy).

Keywords Humanism • Aging • Meaning in life • Well-being • Purpose • Moral worth

A Meaningful Life

Viktor Frankl's *Man's Search for Meaning*, originally published in German in 1946 (Frankl, 2006), has been the main source of inspiration for contemporary research on what makes life meaningful. A representative quote from this book dealing with survival in a concentration camp might be this one: "Any attempt to restore a man's inner strength in the camp had first

© The Author(s), under exclusive license to Springer Nature Switzerland AG 2024
P. Derkx, A. B. Pinn, *Meaningful Aging from a Humanist Perspective*, https://doi.org/10.1007/978-3-031-53869-8_2

to succeed in showing him some future goal. Nietzsche's words, 'He who has a *why* to live for can bear with almost any *how*,' could be the guiding motto (...) Woe to him who saw no more sense in his life, no aim, no purpose, and therefore no point in carrying on. He was soon lost" (Frankl, 2006, p. 76). Important later books on meaning include contributions from philosophy (Klemke & Cahn, 2008; Wolf, 2010; May, 2015; Martela, 2020), psychology (Baumeister, 1991; Wong, 2012; Hicks & Routledge, 2013; Coleman et al., 2015), history (Cole, 1992), cultural anthropology (Mathews, 1996), sociology (Inglis, 2014), and also from interdisciplinary perspectives (Alma & Smaling, 2010; Edmondson, 2015). A glance at these publications shows that there is little agreement on which theory of a meaningful life is the best starting point for further research. 'Meaning *in* life' refers to subjective individual experiences, whereas 'the meaning *of* life' suggests a more objective, transcendent meaning ascribed to human life as a whole. Whereas the latter phrase is used in some philosophical and theological discussions, 'meaning in life' is the term commonly used by social scientists. From now on MIL will be used for 'meaning in life.' Social science publications on 'well-being' and 'quality of life' far outnumber publications on the related but different topic of MIL. 'Well-being' and 'quality of life' seem general enough to include MIL, and all three show substantial overlap. On closer examination, dominant definitions of 'well-being' (Diener, 2009; Ryff, 2014) and 'quality of life' (World Health Organization, 1998) turn out to largely ignore important dimensions of meaning, such as coherence and especially moral worth.

The theory of a meaningful life used in the present text is broad and may apply to *searching* for meaning, *giving* meaning to one's life, *discovering* meaning, or *experiencing* one's life as meaningful. It is also multidimensional. Sometimes a meaningful life is equated with a purposeful life, but most authors (e.g., Baumeister, 1991; Morgan & Farsides, 2009; Martela & Steger, 2016) argue convincingly that a sense of purpose is not the only component of a meaningful life. The theory used in what follows, has been developed by this author and colleagues over a number of years (Derkx, 2011, 2013a, 2015; Derkx et al., 2020) and on the basis of a variety of social-psychological and philosophical sources. It has been used to develop an evaluation standard for the way Dutch care homes deal with existential questions of older people (van der Vaart et al., 2015). The origin of this theory of meaning can be found in the work of social psychologist Roy Baumeister (1991), who suggested four needs that should be satisfied in order to experience life as meaningful. Baumeister's four needs for meaning are needs for *purpose, moral worth* (moral value, moral justification), *self-worth* (self-esteem), and (efficacy or) perceived *control*. Convinced by Mooren (1998), Smaling and Alma (2010), and Morgan and Farsides (2009), respectively, I have added a need for *coherence* (or comprehensibility), a need for *connectedness,* and a need for *excitement* (or wonder). The seven components or dimensions of meaning together sketch the conditions thought to be fulfilled when people experience their lives as meaningful. We will now introduce these dimensions in turn.

- *Purpose*: To have a purpose in life means that someone is able to connect his or her current activities to a valued future state or aspired perspective, to one or more overarching aims and goals that give direction to life.
- *Moral worth* (value or justification): To experience moral worth means one is able to evaluate one's own actions and way of living as morally justified or positively valued in a moral sense. The meaning of 'in a moral or ethical sense' is very controversial among philosophers. Important elements in the debate figure in the following definition of a moral problem: We meet a moral problem when a free subject confronts or evaluates a choice that can be contested or justified on the basis of objective or universal principles which are compelling and which aim at organizing and regulating (a part of) society (van Luijk, 1979, p. 59).
- *Self-worth* (or self-esteem): A feeling of self-worth, including self-respect and self-acceptance, refers to a positive evaluation of oneself. This self-worth is often attained by way of comparison with others, and crucially depends on being socially recognized. In fact, self-worth can also be derived from one's membership of a particular social group that contrasts favorably with other groups.
- *Control*: (Perceived) control pertains to the need to believe that one's life is—to some extent—within one's own control. People need to feel that they are in charge of their lives, that they can make choices that make a difference, that things do not just happen to them. A sense of control, *competence,* and *agency* can not only be achieved by 'real' control but also by what is called *interpretive control*: Understanding what happens generates a sense of control and a change in how the event is experienced, even if the actual event and circumstances are not changed.

- *Coherence* (or comprehensibility): The reality in which one lives needs to be (to some extent) intelligible and well-ordered to perceive life as meaningful. Chaos and fragmentation cause distress and a disruption of meaning. The need for coherence can importantly be satisfied by the creation and maintenance of a life narrative for oneself, which integrates reconstructing and understanding the past, interpreting and evaluating the present, and anticipating and preparing for the future. Such a life story safeguards a stable sense of identity and continuity (McAdams, 1997).
- *Excitement*: The need for excitement, also meant to include wonder or curiosity, describes the importance of elements in our lives that breach the boredom of the usual, that spark our curiosity, that make life interesting. Excitement is the emotional response to things in our lives (for instance a purpose or moral value) that have the power to motivate us to act in a certain direction. Importantly, excitement need not necessarily be caused by positive emotions; imagine political activists fighting injustice or the production and burning of fossil fuels. In a less activist register, excitement can be triggered by an experience of wonder or awe, for example, when one is immersed in nature or art.
- *Connectedness*: Being connected to something other than oneself, refers to having satisfying personal relationships, and to feeling closeness or communion with others or 'the other' in a broad sense. A balance between connectedness (communion) and self-worth and control (agency) is crucial (Bakan, 1966; McAdams, 1997). The need for connectedness need not be restricted to our personal relations with other people. Connectedness can also be expressed in efforts to realize a better society. Moreover, connectedness can also be felt with an impersonal Other, with God, with nature or with another positively valued transcendent reality. (Derkx, 2013a)

These seven dimensions of meaning facilitate fertile reflection and conversation on what makes life meaningful. Thinking, talking, and interviewing about what makes life meaningful in general—so without distinguishing dimensions—often makes people fall silent and results in a more difficult and faltering process. The seven components of meaning are intended to be exhaustive: If all are present to a sufficient degree, a person's life is expected to be meaningful. In contrast, if the seven needs for meaning are not fulfilled, the person involved will expectedly try to adapt their behavior, rearrange priorities, and/or interpret life differently to avoid the threat of meaninglessness. I agree with Baumeister that the number of dimensions or components is somewhat arbitrary and irrelevant. There is quite some overlap between them. What matters most is "the total conceptual space that they cover. (…) The important thing (…) is the totality, not the number of distinctions within it" (Baumeister, 1991, p. 32). Also, particular sources of experienced meaning (such as work, parenthood, or belief in God) often contribute to several needs at the same time.

All worldviews and religions can be interpreted as frameworks that help to satisfy the seven needs for meaning. My personal worldview is a (secular) humanist one, but—like Baumeister's psychological theory—my theory of the seven needs for meaning is meant to be universally human and worldview- or religion-neutral. Of course, it remains to be seen whether this will hold up eventually. In another text—written in co-operation with Hanne Laceulle—I have focused on what makes aging meaningful for humanists. In that text we have elaborated on four defining features of a (secular) *humanist* view of meaningful aging (Derkx & Laceulle, 2021). We define humanism as a meaning frame which has four distinctive (but not exclusive) characteristics: human agency; human dignity; self-realization; and love of vulnerable, unique, and irreplaceable persons.[1] Human agency refers to the epistemological conviction that every meaning frame (whether humanist, atheist, Buddhist, Hindu, Jewish, Christian, Muslim, Marxist, or something else) is a human product that originated in a specific culture and context. The validity of a worldview or religion ultimately is a matter of arguments and considerations introduced and evaluated by humans, individually and socially. A second characteristic is the moral principle that all human beings as citizens ought to regard and treat each other as valuable equals; all human beings have equal dignity, human rights. Third, humanism is characterized by the view that human beings should use their freedom and agency to develop their personal capacities and talents (*Bildung*, self-realization) and to consciously shape their lives according to their goals and values. Thus, if one lets life just happen to them, one should not be called a humanist. A fourth defining feature of humanism, finally, is the assumption that the highest goal of the action and behavior of human individuals should be the love of specific, vulnerable, unique, and for them irreplaceable other persons. This last characteristic arises from historical experiences with egocentric individualism,

---

[1] See also Derkx (2013a).

scientistic utopianism (e.g., Stalinism and its abstract aim of 'the new human' and the ideal communist society), and technocracy (in which for instance a narrowly defined aggregate economic growth is considered more important than the flourishing of human beings individually) (Derkx & Laceulle, 2021, pp. 665–666). It should be noted that the last three defining features of humanism are of a normative, ethical nature.

A humanist view of aging, we think, is in favor of healthy aging and life extension, but human life is and remains inherently vulnerable (not just medically), and in a humanist view other aims are regarded as deserving a higher priority than life extension for privileged social groups with already a high (healthy) life expectancy.[2] Humanist priorities are (1) a better social organization of people's life courses with a better balance among learning, working, caring, and enjoying; (2) more social justice—for too long differences in socio-economic status have been determinants of shocking differences in health and longevity; (3) development and dissemination of cultural narratives that better accommodate the fulfillment of essential meaning-needs of the elderly than the stereotyping decline- and age-defying narratives); (4) less loneliness and social isolation.

Whether this *humanist* view of meaningful aging biases or even invalidates my view of *meaningful* aging for humans in general, is for the reader to judge. In this text my attention focuses on what makes aging meaningful for everybody, whatever their religion or worldview. I will elaborate on the seven dimensions of meaning, both conceptually and empirically, and I will primarily make use of relatively recent publications.

Meaningful Aging: Aging with Purpose

For a meaningful life, one needs a sense of purpose, something to aspire to, to strive for. Some instruments widely used to measure meaning, even equate meaning with purpose: for example, Crumbaugh and Maholick's Purpose in Life Test (PIL, 1967) and Ryff's Purpose in Life Scale (PWB-P, 1989), a subscale of her Psychological Well-Being Scales (Crumbaugh & Maholick, 1967; Ryff, 1989; Morgan & Farsides, 2009, p. 198). A sense of purpose is not the same as simply having a collection of important goals, it is "a superordinate, organizing set of cognitive intentions that provide consistency and flexibility in the pursuit of desired outcomes" (Steger, 2018, p. 5). Examples of purposes in this sense are being a good

[2] See also Derkx (2016).

parent or reducing other people's suffering. With few exceptions, research has shown that sense of purpose declines with age. For older men, consistently higher levels of purpose were found than for older women and a slower rate of decline as they age (Irving et al., 2017, p. 427). In spite of the decline in purpose, the potential to experience purpose remains across the life span. Higher reported purpose has been associated with higher educational level and better health (Pinquart, 2002; Ryff, 2014, p. 14; Irving et al., 2017, p. 427). Whether the correlations of strength of purpose with age, educational level, and health are causal, and in which direction, is not clear.

Human beings have innumerable goals and purposes. Erik Erikson's psychosocial development theory and Laura Carstensen's socioemotional selectivity theory distinguish between different categories of purposes and link them to different stages of a human life. These theories suggest that with age, sense of purpose does not only (or not so much) decline, but changes in character. Erikson's theory of the life cycle distinguishes between pursuing (1) identity goals, by seeking greater autonomy, self-understanding, and self-sufficiency, especially important in adolescence and young adulthood; (2) intimacy goals, by seeking close relationships, especially in young and middle adulthood; (3) generativity goals, by supporting younger generations or contributing to society, especially in middle to old adulthood; and (4) ego-integrity goals, by seeking inner peace and developing a positive view of one's life as a whole, especially in old adulthood (Erikson, 1985). In this way, Erikson presents a developmental sequence of goals: identity goals, intimacy goals, generativity goals, and ego-integrity goals. Erikson has emphasized that goals central in a particular life phase remain relevant in later phases. Thus, intimacy goals and generativity goals remain important in old age, even though ego-integrity goals (coherence) have become central.

The cardinal postulate of Carstensen's socioemotional selectivity theory is that viewing the future as long versus constrained influences goal hierarchies that guide action in daily life. According to socioemotional selectivity theory people have knowledge-seeking goals and emotional meaningfulness goals. Young adults, who often expect to have a long future before them, tend to prioritize knowledge-seeking goals involving exploration and new contacts and experiences, because these 'investments' usually optimize the future. In old adulthood, when the time horizon is perceived as quite limited, people tend to prioritize emotionally meaningful goals and to be more selective in their activities and especially in the people they want to spend time with. They prefer activities and people they already know and like. Socioemotional selectivity theory in this way explains why older adults often are found to have higher (subjective) well-being than younger ones (Carstensen, 1995; Carstensen et al., 1999).

Helene Fung and Carstensen have emphasized that increasing age in itself is not the cause of the shift in purpose from young to old adulthood. They point to a shorter time horizon—also possible for young people under certain conditions—as the direct, underlying cause (Fung & Carstensen, 2006). Justine Irving and others in their literature review also refer to a substantial amount of research suggesting that age in itself is not the effective cause of change or decline in purpose over time. The direct causes, they write, might be age-associated losses, such as of partner, paid work, or social roles. Low sense of purpose for older adults has been attributed to decreased opportunities for purposeful engagement or for continuing roles in society (Irving et al., 2017, p. 429). However, in what sense are the loss of paid work or decreased opportunities for purposeful engagement age-associated? This loss and decline to a considerable part are results of (are caused by) the way we have organized our society and not of the 'natural' process of aging. One of the major impediments to self-realization for older people is the historically contingent social organization of the life course in three consecutive boxes—education, work/childrearing, retirement—and the decline narrative of later life dominant in contemporary Western culture (Dannefer, 1999; Laceulle & Baars, 2014; Derkx & Laceulle, 2021).

These questions of causality refer to the notorious age-period-cohort problem as epistemological riddle. What has been established, when we find that people 80 years of age generally have a lower sense of purpose than people aged 40? Is this because the 80-year-old people are older than the 40-year old people (an age effect)? Is it because the group of 80-year-olds had different formative experiences while growing up, e.g., a devastating economic crisis in the 1930s (a cohort effect)? Or is it because as adults they were influenced for a number of years by a culture in which staying young as long as possible had become the norm and older people were devalued and regarded as a burden, especially after their—in many countries mandatory—retirement (a period effect, which cannot even be circumvented by longitudinal research)? Human aging cannot be studied by itself, in a pure form (Glenn, 2003; Baars, 2010, p. 110). Empirical science is important to provide us with facts and explanations about the situation we are in, but in explanations we should not forget the ever changing social and cultural structures and environments co-determining the recorded facts. Imagine that we would live in a society in which the socially and politically legitimized and supported average life course, for women and men, would be a combination of learning, working, caring, and enjoying from age 15 to 85, and in which the number of hours per week spent in paid employment would be 25 on average between the ages of 20 to 65, and 15 or 10 hours on average between the ages of 15 and 20 and the ages of 65 and 85. Then, in principle, most people would have the possibility to entertain a greater variety of purposes during their whole lives, and we might record very different facts about people's sense of purpose at various ages (Vaupel & Loichinger, 2006; Derkx & Laceulle, 2021).[3]

As regards the relation between aging and purpose, another interesting avenue for further research might be whether people's purposes and time horizons exclusively relate to their own lifetime or transcend it. It seems rather obvious that individuals differ in their concern for future generations and for life after their own death. Less clear is whether this engagement changes with age (period?, cohort?), and if so, how and why. Interesting hypotheses and considerations concerning this question can not only be found in the debate about Erik Erikson's generativity concept but also about Lars Tornstam's gerotranscendence theory (Erikson, [1963] 1986, pp. 266–269; Kotre, 1984; Tornstam, 1997a, p. 143; Schoklitsch & Baumann, 2012; Hofer et al., 2014; Braam et al., 2016; Pratt et al., 2020). More on generativity and gerotranscendence in Section 'Connectedness and Aging: Spirituality.'

MEANINGFUL AGING: MORAL WORTH AND AGING

For the experience of living a meaningful life while aging, one also needs a sense of moral worth, of being able to evaluate one's own personal development, purposes, actions, and way of living as morally justified or positively valued. The need for moral worth seems to cover a large part of what several authors call the need for 'significance' (Janoff-Bulman & Yopyk, 2004; King et al., 2016; Martela & Steger, 2016). Some empirical

---

[3] This issue also relates to the famous 'structural lag' problem as expounded by Riley et al. (1994): social structures lag behind the increase in average life expectancy realized in the twentieth century.

research has been carried out about the relationship between aging on the one hand and values and moral judgment on the other.

The ethical evaluation of one's purpose(s) is, of course, only part of moral worth, but it is an important part. Anne Colby and colleagues regret the tendency of many psychologists to talk about purpose in a functional, content-neutral manner. As if it does not matter whether people have a horrible purpose or an ethically laudable one, as long as they have a sense of purpose. Colby et al. recently published research on purpose beyond the self in later life (Colby et al., 2020). By 'purpose beyond the self' they do not mean purpose beyond one's own life time (beyond the death of the self) but moral purpose, purpose that is not strictly personal but includes a commitment to make a contribution to the well-being of others and the world beyond the self. (Erikson's generativity goals are examples of purpose beyond the self). Colby et al. conducted a US nationally representative survey of 1198 respondents between the ages of 50 and 92, accompanied by in-depth interviews of a number of the survey respondents. The survey revealed that 31% of the respondents is purposeful beyond the self. Female, highly educated, African American, Latino/a, Asian, and mixed-race respondents were a little bit more likely to exhibit moral purpose than male, lower-educated, and white respondents. Participants in the survey were as likely to show moral purpose regardless of age, self-reported income, marital status, retirement status, or self-reported health.[4] And persons (aged 50 to 92) holding moral purpose in high regard do not necessarily neglect their private interest and purposes.

> [C]ontrary to popular preconceptions about people who are strongly committed to the common good, [morally] purposeful respondents do not seem to sacrifice self-oriented pursuits in their later years. They treat engaging beyond the self as entirely compatible with doing fun and interesting things and seeking personal growth. (Colby et al., 2020, p. 12)

These empirical results are in line with a recent normative-ethical argument about and concept of self-realization (self-actualization, self-fulfillment). Philosopher Hanne Laceulle concludes that the purpose of self-realization ought to be moral agency as "an ability that unites four distinct components: (1) to lead a good life (2) with and for others, (3)

---

[4] By definition (see Section 'A Meaningful Life') humanists are purposeful beyond the self. I think many people with other worldviews are as well.

according to one's deepest aspirations and best capacities, (4) as full participating members of a society/community" (Laceulle, 2018, pp. 154–155). Emphasizing that moral agency not only assumes that we strive for a good life *with* others, but also *for* others, implies that the best in human beings (the purpose to be realized in self-realization) includes the ability to engage with the good of others, and through this engagement to realize our own fulfilment (Laceulle, 2018, p. 156).

Colby and colleagues also held lengthy interviews with 102 of their survey respondents. And they compared 18 interviewees who met strict criteria for clear-cut, or exemplary, moral purpose with 18 interviewees who were coded as unambiguously showing no purpose beyond the self, with the groups matched for age and gender. Colby et al. mention a number of interesting findings about the moral purpose exemplars. Many of the older moral purpose exemplars are dealing with their own serious life problems, such as poverty, poor health, family difficulties, and bereavement, but a near-universal level of positivity is visible in this group. They emphasize the joy and satisfaction they experience in their lives, especially their beyond-the-self-engagements. The morally purposeful interviewees also confirm the finding from the survey that their lives are not lives of self-sacrifice. The morally purposeful interviewees more strongly and enthusiastically endorse *both* beyond-the-self *and* self-oriented perspectives on later life than do the non-morally-purposeful respondents. In their analysis of the interviews, Colby et al. also tried to discover what the interviewees are after in life, what is important to them. The researchers found that positive relationships are important sources of satisfaction for both groups of interviewees, but personal relationships were likely to be more positive (fewer references to conflict, betrayal, or alienation) and more central for the respondents with moral purpose. The same was found to be true for excitement, fun, adventure, novelty, or flow as sources of satisfaction. Strong interconnectedness among the sources of satisfaction was highly characteristic of the moral purpose exemplars. Many fewer in the comparison group spoke of the sources of satisfaction as strongly interwoven. Also interesting is, that freedom/autonomy is an important value for both groups, but that the meaning of it is strikingly different in the two groups. For every interviewee without moral purpose who mentioned freedom, freedom had a negative meaning. It was about being free *from* the set schedules of work or (being retired) from certain other responsibilities. For the moral purpose exemplars freedom had a positive meaning. For some it was about now having the freedom *to* stand up for what they really believe in. Some others said they had taken advantage of their freedom from previously time-consuming responsibilities *to* take on more demanding roles aligned with their beyond-the-self purposes. A final point concerns the role of religion. For less than a quarter of the interviewees without moral purpose, spirituality/elevation was important. For half of the interviewees with moral purpose this was the case. However, this also means that for the other half of this group religious faith or spirituality was *not* important, and a significant majority of the interviewees with moral purpose was not driven *primarily* by religious faith (Colby et al., 2020, pp. 12–17). In spite of being drawn from a small number of respondents, this is important information. Baumeister in his *Meanings of Life* (1991) suggested that the decline of religion has created an enormous problem for the fulfilment of needs for meaning, (not only but) especially of the need for moral worth. With Crescioni, Baumeister wrote in 2013:

> While religion offered a set of concrete, largely unchanging values, secular society's values are varied and can shift rapidly. Individuals in modern society receive less guidance regarding right and wrong and are more likely to find themselves uncertain of whether their actions are morally justifiable, as compared to past generations whose religion gave them a sense of universal moral certainty. This value gap is likely to present the greatest challenge to the search for meaning going forward. (2013, pp. 12–13)

I doubt whether religion in premodern society provided people with a sense of shared, absolute, and unchanging moral certainty (see e.g., Ginzburg, 1992), but the interviews by Colby et al. certainly show that religion is not necessary for people being morally motivated. Baumeister and Crescioni conclude that with religion declining in importance, "the world does not seem to have descended into chaos" and "it may be enough for individuals to each find ways to make their own lives seem meaningful" (Crescioni & Baumeister, 2013, p. 13). I think it important that individuals experience moral decisions as not completely arbitrary, but for that it is not necessary that norms and values are eternally unchanging, absolute, or divinely guaranteed. It is enough that human beings in good faith exchange serious arguments and relevant reasons and considerations (Hindriks, 2015).

Shalom H. Schwartz has developed a theory of a comprehensive set of basic human (moral and non-moral) values that are recognized in all societies. The theory defines and orders 19 values on a circular continuum. The placing of the values on the continuum is based on their compatible and conflicting motivations, expression of self-protection versus growth, and personal versus social focus. Older people appear to think certain values are more important than others. Data collected in 2010 show that across representative samples in Finland, Germany, Israel, Italy, New Zealand, Poland, Portugal, Switzerland, Turkey, and the United States (n = 6059) a higher age correlated positively with regarding the following values as more important: (1) conformity to rules, laws, and formal obligations; (2) societal security, order, and stability; (3) preservation of the tradition of one's family, religion, and culture; (4) concern for the welfare of all (including nature). Older adults in the same countries were found to judge certain other values as less important than youth or younger adults: (1) tolerance for different ideas, lifestyles, and groups; (2) dependability, i.e., being available for ingroup members (e.g., children) to rely upon; (3) stimulation, i.e., pursuit of pleasant excitement, novelty, adventures, and experimentation. Again, of course, it is not clear whether the age differences found, are differences due to age, cohort and/or period (Schwartz et al., 2012). And many philosophers will immediately comment: all very well, but … what values *are* most important?

In a study by Karina R. Arutyunova and others, the role of age in moral judgment was explored using survey data collected in Russia (around 2012), the United States, the United Kingdom, and Canada (around 2005). Participants (n = 659) responded to hypothetical moral scenarios describing different situations where sacrificing one life resulted in saving five others. Judging the sacrifice of one life to save five others as permissible (do what is best for the majority) is called a utilitarian response here, judging such a sacrifice as not allowed (do not harm others) is regarded as a deontological judgment. "The analysis of moral judgments across different age groups revealed similar trends within both Russian and Western cultures: the older the age group of participants, the less utilitarian judgments they expressed, and the more they used the non-utilitarian end of the scale ('forbidden')" (Arutyunova et al., 2016, p. 11). Arutyunova and others suggest that this result may reflect developmental processes of accumulation of experience of social interactions throughout the lifespan, leading to an increase in emotional and empathetic involvement in situations with interpersonal context. Recent research by Simon McNair and others in the United States has shown similar results. However, the authors point out that their reported age differences "may reflect a cohort effect driven by generational differences" (McNair et al., 2019, pp. 47–60). The same, of course, might be said of the results presented by Arutyunova and colleagues. My own personal experience provides an important warning. When in the late 1970s I joined the Dutch humanist association 'Humanistisch Verbond,' a vehement moral and political fight was going on about the position the humanist movement ought to take towards the stationing of nuclear cruise missiles in the Netherlands. Many or most of the members of this humanist association had been Christians before they became (secular) humanists. It soon became clear to me that atheistic or agnostic humanists who had formerly been (Calvinist) Protestant Christians overwhelmingly used deontological arguments in the debate, while humanists who had been Roman Catholics used consequentialist, utilitarian arguments. So the differences between utilitarian and deontological judgments might refer to religious conviction, denomination, or worldview and not to age in itself. As a result of sociocultural change, the younger respondents might be less or differently religious. Another factor that might explain why older adults in Arutyunova's sample judge more deontologically and with more empathy is social class. Arutyunova and colleagues did not look at social class, but research by Stéphane Côté et al. shows that upper-class individuals exhibit reduced empathy and are more likely than lower-class participants to make utilitarian moral judgments in dilemmas in which calculated, dispassionate choices are at odds with visceral, deontological moral intuitions (2013).[5]

An important concept in relation to moral worth and aging has been proposed by Malcolm Johnson: biographical pain. Biographical pain is the irremediable anguish which results from profoundly painful recollection of experienced wrongs which can now never be righted, or recollection of deeply regretted actions which cannot be redressed anymore because one is severely impaired or terminally ill (Johnson, 2016, p. 207). The pain and sense of guilt appears to grow in intensity as individuals get closer to death and the opportunity to put things right and to seek or give forgiveness has passed by. Examples of experienced wrongs or regretted actions older people revealed to Johnson as a researcher, are stories (protected and hidden over decades) of: extramarital relations, babies aborted or given up

---

[5] Laceulle (2017) has argued that deontological and utilitarian ethics might be the types of ethics most pertinent to 'the contingent vulnerabilities that threaten later life', but that virtue ethics might be more relevant as far as 'existential vulnerability in later life' is concerned. Existential vulnerability issues (e.g. loss of significant others or a shrinking personal time horizon) cannot be prevented or solved by action. We can only hope to develop a wise response to them (which is more a matter of character development and attitude than of action) and to integrate them meaningfully into our lives.

for adoption whilst husbands fought in a war, sexual and physical abuse by husband or friend, the cheating of a relative or friend out of their business, the break-up of a trusting relationship. Johnson accepts that many older adults show remarkable resilience, but he emphasizes that "we know too little about the anger and guilt, the burning resentments and the unresolved wounds of earlier life and how those near to the end smoulder with injustice at what was done to them—or with self-loathing at what they did to others" (Johnson, 2016, p. 211).

MEANINGFUL AGING: SELF-WORTH AND AGING

In his *Meanings of Life* (1991), Baumeister distinguishes four sub-needs for meaning: the need for purpose, for value (moral worth, justification), for self-worth (self-esteem), and for efficacy (the belief that one has control). I have incorporated these four needs for meaning into my seven-part theory of the experience of a meaningful life. According to Baumeister, the need for self-worth or self-esteem "is to find some basis for positive self-worth. People seek some criteria according to which they can regard themselves and convince others to regard them positively. It is a need to have some claim on respect—both self-respect and the respect of others." And Baumeister adds that, in practice, the need for self-worth "usually takes the form of finding some way to feel superior to others." There is a collective way to feel superior: Emphasizing that one belongs to a superior group that contrasts with a lesser group. And there is an individual way: Emphasizing one's personal achievements within the group one belongs to.

Self-worth overlaps with moral worth (feeling virtuous will not only help to satisfy your need for moral worth but also for self-worth), but there is also a difference between the two. They can even come into conflict. "Among couples contemplating divorce, for example, it is typically a greater blow to one's self-esteem [self-worth] to be abandoned and rejected rather than to be the one to leave; but the leaver suffers the greater guilt [low moral worth]." When divorce draws near, "couples maneuver and manipulate to take responsibility for the breakup (...) Current evidence indicates that people in general seem to prefer to maintain self-worth despite the guilt: After a breakup, more people claim to be the initiator/leaver than the abandoned one," and then they try to justify their departure (the last four quotations are all from Baumeister, 1991, p. 44).

Ulrich Orth, Ruth Yasemin Erol, and Eva C. Luciano recently published a meta-analysis of 191 longitudinal, quantitative empirical studies of self-esteem published between 1975 and 2016 (Orth et al., 2018). The studies reported on 331 independent samples—overwhelmingly from Western countries—with a total of 164,868 participants. The participants were between 4 and 94 years old. To prevent misunderstanding, it is important to point out that like Baumeister Orth et al. report on self-worth in a wide sense (including self-esteem, self-respect, self-acceptance, and similar terms), but contrary to Baumeister they seem to reject the idea that self-worth 'usually' takes the form of finding some way to feel superior to others. Orth and colleagues write: "Self-esteem is defined as a person's subjective evaluation of his or her worth as a person" (2018, p. 1046). They explicitly distinguish self-esteem from narcissism. Self-esteem includes feelings of self-acceptance and a positive attitude toward the self but does not necessarily imply that the individual feels superior to others. While narcissism is characterized by antisocial behavior, a negative view of others, self-centeredness, sense of entitlement, willingness to exploit others, and lack of empathy, high self-esteem is compatible with a prosocial, positive attitude toward others.

The results of the meta-analysis by Orth and colleagues show

> that people's self-esteem changes systematically across the life span. Average levels of self-esteem increased from age 4 to 11, remained stable from age 11 to 15, then increased strongly until age 30 and more slowly until age 60, peaked between age 60 and 70 years, and declined after age 70. (…) The pattern of results did not differ significantly for samples from different birth cohorts and different countries, samples with different compositions in terms of gender and ethnicity, and for different sample types (nationally representative or other), suggesting that the findings are robust and generalizable within Western cultural contexts. (2018, pp. 1063, 1069)

Socioeconomic status, social relationships, and life events might be influential and lead to differences in self-esteem, but information on these factors was unavailable in the majority of the 191 studies. Self-esteem declined after age 70, but the rate of change was small until age 90 and the decline started from a very high level of self-esteem. So the analysis suggests that many old people are able to maintain a relatively high level of self-esteem. Only after age 90 years, self-esteem declined more strongly. However, the estimate for the age group 90–94 years was based on only 2 of the 191 publications. Orth and colleagues refer to research which mentions the following factors that might explain a decrease in self-esteem in old age: loss of social roles as a result of retirement and, possibly, widowhood, and negative changes in social relationships, socioeconomic status, cognitive abilities, and health (2018, p. 1047). Age discrimination or ageism might be involved in these factors (Gullette, 2010, p. 335).

Meaningful Aging: Control and Aging

A sense of control is part of what is necessary for the experience of a meaningful life. Perceptions or beliefs of control (efficacy or mastery) refer to the extent to which a person perceives, senses, or believes he or she has influence over his or her own life (to obtain desired outcomes and to avoid those one does not like). There is much evidence that perceived (subjective) personal control influences a person's behaviors, emotions, well-being, health, and even longevity more strongly than actual (objective) control. Illusions of control often are adaptive biases, as they help people to keep hope and not give up in situations where they feel challenged and perceive uncertainty and risk (Bercovitz et al., 2019; Thompson, 2017; Robinson & Lachman, 2017). Greater control beliefs generally lead to greater engagement in adaptive strategies and health-promoting behaviors resulting in better health, which in turn can lead to increases in perceived control. However, a high sense of control can be harmful when it produces an erroneous sense of omnipotence, invincibility and invulnerability. Knowing when to increase efforts towards control and when to relinquish control may be a form of wisdom (Robinson & Lachman, 2017, p. 441; Thompson, 2017).

Research on perceived control by Jule Specht, Boris Egloff, and Stefan Schmukle using a large and representative sample from the German population (9484 adults between the ages of 16 and 76) gave the following result: cross-sectionally "perceived control increased until approximately ages 30–40, then decreased until approximately age 60, and increased more or less slightly afterwards" (2013, p. 357). Men perceived more control than women in general, but the life course pattern for the sexes was comparable. More highly educated individuals perceived a much higher level of control than less educated individuals. Longitudinally, over the 6-year period from 1999 to 2005, perceived control decreased across all ages. "Besides this difficult-to-interpret main effect, longitudinal results mostly matched the results found cross-sectionally" (Specht et al., 2013,

p. 358). This trajectory of perceived control found in Germany is very similar to the one described for US samples, with one important difference. For Americans, over 60 perceived control declined at an accelerated rate down to an extremely low level, for Germans in this age group a stable or even slightly increasing development in perceived control was found. The explanation offered by Specht et al. draws attention to differences in retirement funding: "individuals in Germany usually experience a relief from hard work when passing into retirement, retirees in the United States frequently have to face poverty" (Specht et al., 2013, p. 360; see also Robinson & Lachman, 2017, p. 436).[6] Strikingly, less educated German individuals (without a degree comparable to high school) showed a stronger rise in perceived control after 60, cross-sectionally as well as longitudinally. Specht et al. explain this by the transition from working life to retirement. More highly educated individuals may have jobs with more room for making their own decisions. It may be quite the opposite for individuals with less education. After retirement, education plays a less prominent role, which is why the difference in experienced level of control between higher and lower educated persons should diminish by then (Specht et al., 2013, p. 362).

One of the better known general frameworks of adaptive development across various periods of the life course, old age being one of them, is the model of "selection, optimization, and compensation" (Freund & Baltes, 1998; Riediger et al., 2006). This framework can be recognized in one of the ways people use to get or keep a sense of control: "older adults maintain a strong sense of general control by deemphasizing the importance of goals that have become difficult to achieve and focusing instead on more reachable goals" (Thompson, 2017, p. 4; see also Wrosch et al., 2012). Another way of acquiring a perception of control in a difficult situation is by *secondary control*. Interpretive control (mentioned above in the introduction of control as one of the components of meaning) is not the same but it seems related to Rothbaum, Weisz, and Snyder's concept of secondary control. Primary control is the belief that one can get desired outcomes and avoid those one does not like, secondary control "involves accepting one's life circumstances as they are, instead of working to change them" (Thompson, 2017, p. 4). Acceptance can be achieved in a variety of ways, including comparison with others in a situation that is worse, and

---

[6] A historical note is relevant here: in 2004 German state pensions have been reduced and more German retirees live in poverty now.

finding benefits and meaning in a loss and in a difficult life situation. An example of the latter was found in stroke patients who reported that their stroke helped them appreciate life and their spouse and that they have grown from the experience. Perceived control can also be promoted and hindered by one's social environment. Receiving support from other individuals, the perception that one can effectively engage others' help, and empathic reactions of others to one's plight, can all contribute to a sense of personal control that is independent of the contribution of personal agency. Control perceptions differ by culture and ethnicity. Both Asian-Americans and Asians in Asia have lower levels of perceived control than do non-Asians in the United States (Thompson, 2017, pp. 5 and 9).

The last two sections have shown relations between control and purpose, control and coherence (comprehensibility), and control and connectedness. Different components of MIL seem to be linked to each other in significant ways.

Meaning Aging: Coherence and Aging

Coherence or comprehensibility is an important dimension of the experience of life as meaningful. Many authors emphasize this (van Praag, 1982; Mooren, 1998; Janoff-Bulman & Yopyk, 2004; Heintzelman et al., 2013; King et al., 2016; Martela & Steger, 2016). Coherence, as already indicated above, is the opposite of chaos, fragmentation, and discontinuity. In the context of MIL, Samantha Heintzelman, Jason Trent, and Laura King have done research on the cognitive component of the sense of coherence,[7] which they describe as possessing knowledge of reliable connections and patterns in the environment (useful for evolutionary adaptation and survival). In the way of experimental psychology Heintzelman et al. try to answer the question whether self-reports of a meaningful life reflect experiences with reliable pattern or coherence in objective reality. For example,

---

[7] By 'sense of coherence' I do not refer here to the broader theoretical construct developed by Aaron Antonovsky in his salutogenic model of health. Antonovsky's 'sense of coherence' consists of three components: (cognitive) comprehensibility, (instrumental/behavioral) manageability and (emotional) meaningfulness. Comprehensibility (the stimuli from one's internal and external environments in the course of living are structured, predictable, and explicable) more or less concurs with the cognitive side of coherence as discussed in this chapter. Antonovsky himself opposed lifting individual dimensions out of his sense of coherence construct in order to examine them separately. See Antonovsky (1987) and Eriksson (2017).

after reading a triad of opaquely coherent words ('magic, plush, floor,' common associate: carpet) research participants completing a survey about their experienced 'meaning' and 'purpose' reported higher MIL than the members of a control group which had read an incoherent triad of words ('magic, actor, spoon'). When people are exposed to pattern or coherence, their experience of MIL increases or when they are exposed to randomness or incoherence their MIL is reduced (Heintzelman et al., 2013). Heintzelman et al. do not deny that the level of experienced existential meaning is influenced by other variables than a sense of cognitive coherence. All they claim is that detecting objective coherence in one's environment influences MIL to some extent. MIL ratings "at least in part, reflect the coherence that characterizes one's world at any given moment" (Heintzelman et al., 2013, p. 996).

Several authors have written about coherence in a wider sense. In Jan Hein Mooren's view, coherence presupposes a worldview: A representation of reality and of why developments and events occur as they do (referring to plausible causes and reasons). When explanations for what happens fit with or do not contradict one's worldview, one lives in a comprehensible world (Mooren, 1998, pp. 199, 203). An exceptionally important part of the world, of course, is one's own self and one's evolving life. The creation and maintenance of a personal life narrative is a crucial way to promote one's sense of coherence. Interestingly, Erik Erikson links his concept of ego-integrity to "a sense of *coherence* and *wholeness*" (Erikson & Erikson, 1998, p. 65). In the words of Andreas Kruse and Eric Schmitt:

> Even back in adolescence, people begin to create a coherent life story that—in normal circumstances—becomes more and more a definite story, a basis for reconstructing and understanding the past, for interpreting and evaluating the present, as well as for anticipating the future, setting aims, making plans, and goal pursuit and goal adjustment. (2019, p. 433)

In Erikson's psychosocial development theory establishing ego-integrity is an indispensable task at the end of human life—if people do not succeed in this task, they are expected to suffer from despair and feelings of disgust about their own lives. As Kruse and Schmitt write: "Ego-integrity is conceptualized as a positive ending point of lifelong identity development (…) Achieving ego-integrity implies being able to accept one's life as a whole, including lost opportunities and unfulfilled aspirations and expectations" (2019, p. 434; see Malcolm Johnson's 'biographical pain').

Despairing persons are depressed about disappointments and missed chances in life. They frequently express sadness, regret, or failure, often in the form of sarcastic remarks implying a sense of futility, triviality, or a low opinion of oneself (paraphrasing S. Hearn et al., 2012, quoted by Kruse & Schmitt, 2019, p. 433). Thus (lack of) coherence not only refers to (difficulty in) creating a life narrative that is cognitively/intellectually comprehensible, but also one that is emotionally acceptable. I think something similar will go for the worldview Mooren writes about. The coherence of the narrative about the social and physical world one lives in, not only refers to intellectual comprehensibility but also to emotional acceptability.

For some time, debates have been going on about the extent to which coherence is necessary and even possible. Social psychologist Baumeister deals with this issue in terms of what he calls "the myth of higher meaning". According to him:

> Meanings of life are actually built up in small chunks. People make sense of their lives one day at a time. Each action, each day, may be meaningful, and as one gets older one thinks in terms of longer and longer units (…) The temptation is to think that one's entire life fits into a single, coherent pattern—that it fits into a life story. (Baumeister, 1991, p. 60)

The myth of higher meaning promises that all parts of and events in life fit together somehow (like the pieces of a jigsaw puzzle), and it is a myth because not everything does fit together (some pieces of the puzzle of life do not fit and some pieces may be lacking).

> The effort to fit everything into one story may fail; each life has several main stories. The story of your career may have only a minor, trivial relation to the story of your marriage. And even these main stories fail to encompass everything that happens. Each day may have moments that (…) are irrelevant and perhaps even contradictory to the main themes of a person's life. (Baumeister, 1991, pp. 60–61)

Baumeister asserts that people desire coherence, and that this desire makes them exaggerate the actual coherence in life. He distinguishes three facets in the myth of higher meaning. One part of the myth is the assumption of *completeness*, the idea that everything makes sense, that all fits together: Every dilemma can be resolved and every decision has a best (or least bad) option. Another part of the myth of higher meaning is the assumption of *consistency*. The desire for consistency has been well documented by psychologists. The myth is the illusion that the answers to different problems never contradict each other and, e.g., that moral values and principles never make opposite demands for how to act.[8] A third aspect of the myth of higher meaning concerns false claims of permanence and *stability*. People use meaning to create stability, continuity, identity, but in doing so they often overestimate stability. Marriage, for example, is the imposition of a stable structure ('till death do us part') onto a changing pattern of acts and feelings. The meaning imposed, however, also operates to increase the actual stability.

Mark Freeman stresses context. Life stories are always told in a trio of contexts: an intersubjective, a larger autobiographical and a socio-cultural context. Without these contexts, fragmentary tales told by people with dementia, for example, will sound incoherent indeed. Often, however, the stories of people without impairments will only make sense in context as well. Freeman has also emphasized that a person's life narrative and the messy process of 'life itself' do not form a binary opposition. The autobiographical stories someone tells others and him- or herself, function in and have effect on the course of that person's life. And narratives need not flatten out all difference, discontinuity, and confusion and are not to be understood merely as a mechanism creating "(an illusory) unity, harmony, and closure amidst the chaotic openness of reality" (Freeman, 2010, p. 171).

In philosophy the degree to which coherence in an individual life story is necessary or even desirable has been discussed in terms of narrative integration and unified personhood. Hanne Laceulle starts her overview of the debate with the remark that "the idea that our lives should, or even could, form fully coherent narrative 'wholes,' or that such unity is a necessary condition for experiencing a meaningful life, is rightly questioned" (Laceulle, 2018, p. 132). We are not only agents organizing and structuring our life story, we are also enjoying, suffering, or enduring things that are not planned by us but happen to us. Laceulle's survey of the philosophical debate—with Dieter Thomä and Margaret Urban Walker as primary participants—concludes with a view of a more modest and flexible

---

[8] Isaiah Berlin has convincingly argued that moral values often clash with each other, and that a perfect society therefore cannot exist. Modestly, we have to keep balancing (Berlin, 1991). I see no reason to think that the human condition is different for individuals.

narrative integration which is very much in line with the psychological views of Baumeister and Freeman.

> Our lives and selves are built of multiple storylines. Some of them cover large parts of our lives, others only short episodes. Some of our storylines fit together harmoniously, while others may be conflictive. None of these storylines encompasses the entirety of who we are (…) Still (…) the different storylines (…) need to interact in such a way that enough coherence emerges to "get by with ourselves". Only then can narrative agents experience and present their life and self as a meaningful configuration. The resulting integration will always be a vulnerable, partial, fragmented and temporary constellation, but one that is nevertheless indispensable. (Laceulle, 2018, p. 134)

Without some sense of coherent selfhood, people do not have a perspective from which to perceive, deliberate, and act. Psychological and philosophical research leads to the conclusion that coherence and ego-integrity are more about being able, cognitively and emotionally, to accept one's life as a whole, than about finding complete and ever-lasting intellectual unity and consistency in one's life story. As the Dutch humanist J. P. van Praag wrote, a meaningful life is not about an all-encompassing vision of life and death, but about coherence in life experiences (van Praag, 1982, chapter 4). Baumeister, Freeman, and Laceulle are one in the conclusion that even amidst all convincing arguments against complete, unitary, linear, and everlasting integration of life stories, some kind of coherence is looked for by almost all people. Most people look for something that binds together, however loosely, the heterogeneous elements of the life they have lived and the life they want to live.

MEANINGFUL AGING: EXCITEMENT AND AGING

In 2009, Jessica Morgan and Tom Farsides published an article which used factor analysis to identify the latent constructs underlying three popular MIL measures (2009).[9] They found five constructs and four of these more or less concur with dimensions of meaning dealt with here above: purpose, coherence, control, and self-worth/moral worth. The fifth one they found is excitement. I agree with Morgan and Farsides that a

---

[9] The three measures are: J. C. Crumbaugh and L. T. Maholick's Purpose in Life Test (1967), J. Battista and R. Almond's Life Regard Index (1973) and C.D. Ryff's Purpose in Life subscale of her Psychological Well-Being scale (1989).

meaningful life in a way also will be an exciting life. 'Exciting' may not be a very adequate term to catch what is meant, but I do not know a better one. With Morgan and Farsides, 'exciting' denotes and connotes new, unknown, different, interesting. I already indicated above that curiosity, wonder, and awe can also be regarded as part of excitement. The opposite of exciting is boring, dull, more-of-the-same, routine. In his seminal study, Frankl already dealt with boredom as the main manifestation of meaninglessness or, as he also calls it, the experience of an inner emptiness, an "existential vacuum" (Frankl, 2006, p. 106). Amanda Melton and Stefan Schulenberg have published research showing that there exists "a strong, significant negative correlation" between the scores on the Purpose in Life test (meant to be measuring meaning) and the Boredom Proneness Scale (2007, p. 1016). They even admit that the correlation is so strong that it might be argued that the two scales measure the same construct, and that lack of boredom is a component of meaning by definition. It is certainly plausible that having purposes is one of the ways in which life becomes interesting.

There has been empirical research on the relation between aging and excitement in the sense of a high-arousal positive (and negative?) emotional state. High- and low-arousal states differ, e.g., in rate of heartbeat and rate and depth of breathing. An association has been found between older adulthood on the one hand and on the other hand *increases* in the experience of low-arousal emotional states, *increases* in the pleasantness of low-arousal states (feeling calm, serene, relaxed), *decreases* in physiological arousal, and *decreases* in the pleasantness of (negative as well as positive) high-arousal states such as fear, hostility, nervousness, excitement, enthusiasm, and elation (Tsai et al., 2018, p. 976). Going on from this, Jeanne Tsai et al. in two recent studies with 849 and 164 younger, middle-aged, and older adults found confirmation for their hypothesis on *ideal* affect. Their results confirmed that the more people *value* excitement and other high-arousal positive states, the less they will look forward to and the more they will dread their own old age (defined as 75 or older) (Tsai et al., 2018, p. 987). Tsai et al. also succeeded in showing links with culture. They found remarkable cross-cultural consistency between age and *actually experienced* affect. Among European American adults, Chinese American adults, as well as Hong Kong Chinese adults, older adults experienced low-arousal positive states more and (high-arousal and low-arousal) negative emotional states less than did younger adults. There were no age differences in actual experiences of high-arousal positive states. However, a difference between cultures was found when *ideal* affect was studied. European American older adults (relatively healthy and most of them not very old) *valued* high-arousal positive states as much as their younger counterparts, while Hong Kong Chinese and Chinese American older adults valued high-arousal positive states less than did their younger counterparts. Older European Americans valued high-arousal and low-arousal positive states more than older Chinese Americans and Hong Kong Chinese. The relation with factors like health status and being very old is still unclear, but Tsai et al. wonder whether Chinese American and Hong Kong Chinese older adults have a higher acceptance of age-related changes in affective experience than European Americans. Higher acceptance of actual emotional experience might lead to decreases in ideal affect (Tsai et al., 2018, p. 988).

Tsai et al. reduce excitement to high-arousal emotional states. As a component of meaning, however, excitement is broader. It is not only related to unique, extreme, or spectacular achievements or events. In an interesting study published in 2020, Jacky van de Goor, Anneke Sools, Gerben Westerhof, and Ernst Bohlmeijer executed research in which they linked 'meaningful moments' with 'emotions of wonder.' They used the 'Wonderful Life question' to elicit narratives of most important life moments from 100 participants varying in age, profession, and social status (van de Goor et al., 2020, p. 147). The Wonderful Life question instigates a concentrated and concise form of life review and reads as follows: "What if there is an afterlife. There, all your memories will be erased, except for one. Which memory do you choose to take with you to eternity?" (van de Goor et al., 2020, p. 154). Because participants can take only one memory to eternity, the authors plausibly assume that the selected memories must be very meaningful. Participants were asked to tell their memory like a film fragment of their life, giving as much detail as possible, but without explaining their choice or describing the wider context of the memory. To qualitatively analyze the narratives of the meaningful moments, van de Goor et al. used characteristics of emotions of wonder (or enchantment, awe, or being moved) as found in the wonder literature. What moments of wonder have in common is their extraordinariness. They are extraordinary in the sense of *sticking out* (as new and unique or positive) *from the* (known and familiar or negative) *context* in which they are experienced. Or they are extraordinary in the sense of being the result of surprising *coincidence or chance or*, the opposite, induced by *intentional focus and awareness*. Regarding this focus and awareness, van de Goor et al. remark that in such cases situations are deliberately created to be extraordinary (weddings, for example) or the extraordinary becomes visible within the ordinary because of an intentional mind-set. A particular intentional mind-set may make interesting and wonderful what otherwise would be boring, dull repetition. Examples are the regular walk in the park, watching a baby sleeping, bedtime or weekend breakfast rituals, coming home after a day's work. It might be so that in general people tend to ascribe less meaning to minor, trivial events (King & Hicks, 2009), the study by van de Goor et al., however, shows that regular and perfectly normal moments can be experienced as extraordinary and extremely meaningful.

The study by van de Goor et al. suggests that excitement as a component of meaning does not always refer to a high-arousal positive emotional state and, even more, that the opposition between excitement and repetition, routine does not hold. In a related study, van de Goor et al. address "the paradox that familiar routines entail": Familiar, recurring routines may be taken for granted and contribute to feelings of indifference, but they may also become meaningful and produce wonder and enchantment (van de Goor et al., 2019, p. 293). In ordinary routines, the extraordinary can become visible. How does this work? On the basis of their research with the Wonderful Life question, van de Goor et al. distinguish two types of familiar routines that produce meaning: routines of transition and routines of harmony.

The following is an example of a memory of a routine of transition that a middle-aged woman wanted to take with her into the afterlife:

> My moment, well, imagine, I … I have a boat. And I am on this boat, it's a sailboat, about 11 meters long. My family is on board, two daughters, my husband. And … we are going on holiday, and then we … usually, when the weather is good, we set onto the ocean, so it is clear blue weather, a nice breeze, we navigate into the sluice here in IJmuiden, and after that the sluice opens, the sail is raised. You hear the seagulls, and the sun. And the … the moment the motor is turned off, that is the moment I would like to take. You know, just the sail, and me at the rudder, and the rest, well, yes they're on board, but that's of secondary importance. Raising the sail, yes, that moment. (van de Goor et al., 2019, pp. 302–303)

On analysis, the routine instrumental act of raising the sail here transforms the situation and produces a transition toward an extraordinary positive experience, the experience of freedom and autonomy (van de Goor et al. call this an experience of a higher purpose, higher than merely sailing onto the sea).

And here is an example of a memory of a routine of harmony, chosen for eternity by a woman in her mid-20s:

> I choose the moment that I step out of the car with my two sisters and my father, at one of our meadows, cornfields, at the end of a beautiful summer day. We are in the twilight, it is still comfortably warm, the atmosphere is calm and safe. This was a custom that occurred several times a week in the summer months: My father often took us to see how the grasslands and corn were doing at the end of the day. There, we played calmly in nature, in our dresses and boots. Around us the sounds of grazing cows, a summer breeze, humming insects, the car radio in the background. The feeling of connection to each other, to the soil that my parents worked, and freedom from the rest of the world. I think I was around eight years old. (van de Goor et al., 2019, p. 303)

Reflecting on these examples of ordinary but meaningful routines and on what we know about the relation between aging and arousal states and between aging and affect, one may be seduced into thinking (1) that routines of transition and routines of harmony represent low-arousal states of excitement in which ordinary, regularly occurring events have become highly meaningful and are far from dull and boring, and (2) that routines of transition and harmony are certainly not the exclusive prerogative of older people but—given the fact that older people experience more low-arousal positive states and experience them as more pleasant—these routines are especially fitting for them as ways to experience life as exciting and meaningful, and (3) that the fear of many people of their own old age might be related to an over-appreciation of the high-arousal kind of excitement and to an underestimation of the possibility of seeing the extraordinary in the usual. Perhaps in the course of their lives older people more often than younger ones have developed a mind-set to get excited about what on the surface appears common and ordinary.

Meaningful Aging: Connectedness and Aging—Personal Relationships

The last (but not least important) dimension of meaning, in my theory, is connectedness. Connectedness, of course, primarily refers to love. Robert Sternberg distinguishes between three 'components' of love: passion, companionship, and commitment. In (stages of) personal relationships, the emphasis on components can differ and components can be combined in different ways (Sternberg, 1986). There is ample evidence that love of partner, child, parent, family member, and friend is a potent source of meaning, not just in the sense of connectedness, but also in most of its other dimensions, especially purpose and moral worth (Baumeister, *Meanings of Life*, Chapter 7, 'Passionate Love, Domestic Bliss'; Stillman & Lambert, 2013).

The substantial increase in life expectancy during the last 150 years has meant that spouses and other life partners have a better chance of spending many years together while being old. It also means that they may realistically expect to take part in the lives of their adult children, if any. And it also means that they might get to know grandchildren or even great-grandchildren. Other societal developments such as de-traditionalization (individualization), higher mobility, women's emancipation, and the rise of information and computer technology, have resulted in "less obligatory and rigid and more flexible and voluntary" personal relationships.

> In late modern society family ties are based less on traditional rules of belonging, on "natural" feelings of duty and obligation. By contrast, the significance of friendship and other informal relationships has increased. (…) People are less able to fall back on "given" bonds such as family or neighborhood relationships. (Machielse & Hortulanus, 2013, pp. 123–124)

Friends have become more important, although the social and legal status of friends has remained quite different from family members (de Vries, 2010). In addition, comparison of 25 European countries has shown that socioeconomic position (sufficient current income), and the availability of appropriate social welfare policies for those in need are crucial country-level conditions for the alleviation of loneliness (Fokkema et al., 2012). So in spite of the personal and intimate character that relationships of family and friendship mostly have, they are influenced by (changes in) social conditions and are not just, as Antonucci and Webster state, "a naturally occurring phenomenon (...) accessible and available to all" (Antonucci & Webster, 2019, p. 477).

Over the course of our lives, the size of social networks first increases and then decreases, peaking at around age 40–50. Young people actively seek to expand their social connections.

> As people get older, they begin to exhibit a stronger desire to seek meaning in their lives, the urgency of which is partly driven by their realization of the diminishing time left in their lives (...). Older adults eliminate less-essential relationships and connections and focus more on relationships that bring more meaning and joy in a process known as "social network pruning." Consequently, older people appear to have smaller but more emotionally rich social networks than younger people. (Streeter et al., 2016, section 1.1)

Stereotypically, older people often are lonely, in the sense that they have the unpleasant experience that their network of relationships is felt to be deficient in some important way (their social network does not fulfill their needs for practical, emotional, and companionship support). Therefore it is important to note that surveys in Europe and North America between 1980 and 2000 have shown that loneliness between the ages of 45 and 79 (20% to 36% often feel lonely) is lower than between the ages of 15 and 24 (31% to 51%). Loneliness is common among the young and among people over the age of 80 (39% to 49%) (Dykstra, 2009). Research in the Netherlands by Roelof Hortulanus, Anja Machielse, and others found that around 2005 the percentage of lonely people between the ages of 18 and 70 was between 24 and 31%. Between the ages of 71 and 80 43% often felt lonely and at the age of 81 and over 46% felt lonely. The higher percentages for the people over 70 can be explained by the fact that they are more frequently struck by major negative life events such as the death of a beloved person (partner, friend, sibling, or otherwise) or by a deteriorating health condition (Machielse & Hortulanus, 2013). These data represent serious social problems, but one should not ignore that they also show that about 55% of the people over 70 are *not* lonely.[10]

---

[10] Longitudinal research by Pearl Dykstra and others has shown that loneliness among older persons can also decrease as a result of new partnerships, new commitments after retirement, increased interactions with children and grandchildren, and improvement in health; see Dykstra et al. (2005)).

Interviews indicate that loving parents and a happy youth provide important protection against loneliness, a whole life long. Factors that play a negative role in the lives of lonely individuals are: lack of attention and love during one's youth, the loss of someone close, a serious illness of oneself or an important other, conflict-ridden relationships or the inability to find a suitable partner, carrying a secret, having little education, problems at work, incapacity for work, and retirement. It is not obvious what is cause or consequence, but these negative factors are often accompanied by a lack of personal competencies. For developing and maintaining a satisfactory social network, especially in late modern society, certain competencies are helpful, if not necessary: sufficient self-respect, ability to overcome feelings of fear, guilt, and shame, daring to show one's vulnerability, the ability to take the initiative, to bring about a situation that is perceived as meaningful, and to search for alternatives if the situation does not satisfy. The development of competencies continues during a person's entire life course, but it seems likely that the possibility to experience connectedness and love in old age in many cases depends on having had a good enough youth (Machielse & Hortulanus, 2013).

Assuming that between 30% and 50% of the people over the age of 70 often feel lonely, we now ask what the consequences are for a meaningful life. It will be obvious that feeling lonely points to a lack of connectedness and companionate (and passionate) love. One may still love a deceased partner or friend, and the memories might remain important and meaningful, but the intimacy and connectedness this relationship provided will often also be more painful than meaningful. The situation after a divorce is different, of course, but memories and meaning effects then will also be mixed, if not more negative.

Research has shown that the effect of loneliness on health and on risk of premature death is strikingly large. "For instance, the risk associated with lacking social connectedness is equivalent to smoking up to fifteen cigarettes per day, and is greater than alcohol abuse, physical inactivity (sedentary lifestyle), obesity, and air pollution" (Holt-Lunstad, 2018, pp. 450–451). But health is not everything and social connectedness and meaning are sometimes regarded as more important in themselves. In a study of people over the age of 85 in the Netherlands, it turned out that these really old people viewed deterioration of physical functioning as normal, something to be expected because of their chronological age. They regarded adaptation to physical and mental limitations and losses as more important than preventing limitations and losses. It is as if physical and cognitive functioning is regarded as very important, as long as people are younger. For the very old the hierarchy has changed. Social contacts are regarded as much more important than physical and cognitive health. Physical and cognitive functioning is no longer essential in itself but instead is perceived as the means for functioning on a desired social level (von Faber et al., 2001; see also Shmotkin et al., 2013).

The following case from the same Dutch study attests to the importance of love, not just of positive social relationships.

> Klaas and Vera Philipsen [not their real names] are well-to-do, live in a beautiful house with a garden, and have many social contacts. Their ability to stay in control and to adjust to old age is well illustrated in their decision to adopt a young dog. When the anthropologist (M.F.) asked Ms Philipsen whether she regarded herself as successful in her life, she said she was not. Years ago, there had been a conflict between her husband and her daughter. At the time, she chose her husband's side and since that incident the daughter has severed all contacts with them. The fact that she has lost all contact with her daughter gives her a continuing feeling of loss. All her successes in life are overshadowed by this failure. (von Faber et al., 2001, p. 2697)

Adaptation to old age seems to have been successful, but adaptation to losing her daughter has turned out impossible. It is hard to imagine that this does not harm her sense of meaning in life. Connectedness, positive social relationships, and companionate love are important for physical and mental health, but they are also essential for experiencing life as meaningful.

Meaningful Aging: Connectedness and Aging—Spirituality

As mentioned in the first section of this text, connectedness not only refers to personal relations with other people. The self can be transcended in many different ways. The idea of connectedness becomes wider when one feels a desire and duty to contribute to a more just and sustainable society, to the well-being of future generations, and even more so if one feels connected with an impersonal Other, with God and/or with nature. In this context, the debate about aging and spirituality becomes relevant (Atchley, 2009; Laceulle, 2013; Johnson & Walker, 2016). Although many different definitions of spirituality exist,[11] most of these definitions agree that spirituality is about a connection with something that is larger than the individual human being, a transcendent realm that might, but need not necessarily be interpreted along religious lines (Coleman et al., 2011; Edmondson, 2015; Fowler, 2015; MacKinlay, 2016; Derkx, 2018; Kruse & Schmitt, 2019). The Belgian philosopher Leo Apostel has argued persuasively that spirituality is also important for atheists, and he has proposed a universally human definition of spirituality. According to Apostel, what happens in any form of spirituality essentially comes down to two processes. In spirituality, one is (a) consciously situating oneself within the largest whole to which one considers oneself to belong, and (b) orientating oneself to the ultimate goals one wants to serve in one's life (Apostel, 1998).

Two research topics in aging research are definitely relevant in the context of spirituality: generativity and gerotranscendence. Erik Erikson was the first to use the term *generativity* in a psychological sense. (In Section 'Aging with Purpose' we already wrote about the importance of generativity goals in middle and old age.) Ed de St. Aubin provides a useful summary of Erikson's ideas about generativity. In Erikson's life cycle model of human development the first five stages result, if successfully traversed, in the growth of competencies and abilities of the self. But in the sixth stage, characterized by a tension of *Intimacy* vs. *Isolation*, the young adult seeks to invest in the well-being of another person, a romantic life partner. The psychological virtue developed in this stage is love.

> This developmental shift to other-orientedness allows for *care*, the psychosocial virtue associated with the successful resolution of the *Generativity vs. Stagnation* tension experienced in the lengthy years of midlife [the seventh stage, roughly from 30 to 65]. The beneficiary, or target, of generative efforts is much wider than the single romantic other of the [sixth] stage. Now the adult seeks to benefit (though not always consciously) future humankind. (…) Erikson's [eighth,] final life cycle stage portrays the elder as having moved back again to a more self-based tension as one attempts to find a favourable balance of *ego integrity* (acceptance of one's lived life and of one's inevitable death) over *ego despair* (unfavourable review of one's life and inability to face death). (…) The successful resolution of this final

---

[11] In Section 'Moral Worth and Aging' I have already referred to spirituality as discussed by Anne Colby et al. (2020). It is not clear to me what definition of spirituality they use.

psychosocial stage depends, in part, on one's earlier generativity (...). (de St. Aubin, 2013, pp. 242–243)

Generativity involves two broad motives: caring for and contributing to future generations, as well as a wish to leave a legacy of the self in doing so. The first motive expresses a sense of connectedness and communion (handing out a gift), the second motive relates to control and agency (creating a gift). A widely used measure of generative concern is the Loyola Generativity Scale (LGS). Generativity can manifest itself in a wide variety of actions and behaviors. De St. Aubin mentions creating pieces of art, attempting to instill important values in one's children, donating money to good causes, and minimizing one's carbon footprint. Michael W. Pratt et al. recently published a review of research on Erikson's generativity concept over the adult life span. They refer to studies showing that generativity was a salient theme with environmental activists, and that these activists felt connected with the future of the world's ecosystems as well as with future human generations. Environmental activists with higher scores on the LGS could successfully be predicted to have a stronger environmental engagement (Pratt et al., 2020, p. 14). Generativity is the hallmark of the psychosocial healthy adult in Erikson's theory. A study using the large (8000+), representative longitudinal MIDUS sample from the United States, showed that greater generativity in midlife predicted more cognitive-evaluative satisfaction with retirement 10 and 20 years later (Pratt et al., 2020, p. 8). The generative output of individuals not just increases their well-being, it also contributes to a better environment and society. A person's generative efforts connect them to something larger than themselves, and this connectedness provides meaning. If generative concerns, goals, and actions are part of a conscious and regularly sustained practice, they are part of a spiritual way of life.

Generativity is not only or not even primarily important in midlife: "this presumably midlife construct in fact shows an important and meaningful presence across the entire adult life span" (Pratt et al., 2020, p. 16). Research using the MIDUS sample (initially aged 25–75) found very limited mean changes over a 10-year follow-up among any of the age groups (Pratt et al., 2020, pp. 3–4). Erikson himself coined the term "grand-generativity" for a type of generativity found in grandparents. Different components of generativity may come to the fore at different stages of personality development. Generative *concerns and desires* may be prominent early in the life course, while generative *actions or feelings of accomplishment* may figure later in life (Pratt et al., 2020, p. 4). Cohort differences might also develop over time. By improved health and education the average 80 year old adult nowadays might, for instance, be different in generativity concerns, actions, and possibilities from their counterparts 50 years ago (Pratt et al., 2020, p. 6). So, instead of being a characteristic of a particular phase in the life of human beings, generativity might, empirically, be more like a stable personality trait of some people and not (or less) of others (Pratt et al., 2020, p. 4).

Of course, and although the pathway for parent to child transmission of prosocial qualities might often be genetic as well (Pratt et al., 2020, p. 17), this does not detract from the idea that it would be good for all human beings, societies, and our environment, if the development of generativity would be a normal and normative part of parenting, education, socialization, community building, and civic programming. Gruenewald et al. executed an experimental study with older adults (mean age 67 years) which is interesting here. The researchers randomly assigned participants to an intergenerational helping program in the Baltimore public schools versus to a control group. The program involved helping with classroom needs and other daily tasks and was several months in length. Results showed lasting effects of helping the school children in terms of increased generative desire and activity over a 2-year follow-up period (Pratt et al., 2020, p. 9). So generativity can be learned, even still by older adults. Generativity and civic engagement mutually foster each other. And they contribute to a meaningful life because they contribute to a sense of purpose, excitement, moral worth, self-worth, control, coherence, and connectedness.

Lars Tornstam's theory of '*gerotranscendence*' is another of the better researched and discussed theories linking aging and spirituality. Gerotranscendence is defined as "a shift in metaperspective, from a materialistic and pragmatic view of the world to a more cosmic and transcendent one, normally accompanied by an increase in life satisfaction" (Tornstam, 1997a, p. 143). The gerotranscendence concept is divided in three dimensions: a cosmic dimension, a self-dimension, and a social-relational dimension. On the cosmic dimension, people qualifying as gerotranscendent experience a new sense of connectedness or even unity with the universe, a sense of being part of a larger cycle of generations (past, present, and future), and a high acceptance of the mysteries of life. On the self-dimension, gerotranscendent individuals show a decrease in self-centeredness, recognition of shadow sides in their personality, and a sense of what Erik Erikson termed 'ego-integrity' and what we have discussed above as coherence (Tornstam, 1997b, 2005; Erikson & Erikson, 1998; Braam et al., 2016). On the social-relational dimension, gerotranscendent individuals feel a transformation of their contacts with other people, such as preferring deeper relationships with a few people rather than more superficial relationships with many people,[12] and a transcendence of the need to follow social conventions. Developing gerotranscendence on these three dimensions implies that people redefine their understanding of themselves, revalue their relationships with other people, and deepen their sense of connection with the universe (Ahmadi Lewin, 2001; Kruse & Schmitt, 2019). In terms of meaning-needs, gerotranscendence stimulates a reconsideration of purposes, ethical commitments and values, connectedness they feel with others and with the cosmos, and a deepening reflection on one's sources of self-worth. Also, the spiritual experience that is associated with the development of gerotranscendence may give rise to feelings of wonder and excitement that form a highly important component of meaning as well, which we have treated earlier in this text. It should be noted, however, that Tornstam's respondents report a decrease in the need to feel in charge of one's life. Other, longitudinal research by Braam et al. confirms this: Low levels of mastery is significantly correlated with cosmic transcendence (Braam et al., 2016). This raises interesting questions regarding the possibly shifting importance of the need for control for people developing 'gero'transcendence.

As the phrase 'gero' in 'gerotranscendence' indicates, Tornstam's theory is based on the premise that this is a form of spiritual development that is specific to later life. Empirical studies using measurements of gerotranscendence, however, have shown that the indicated fundamental shift in life perspective seems to be connected more with having experienced certain influential life events (such as existential losses) than with chronological age as such (Tornstam, 1997b, 2005; Braam et al., 2016). As with generativity, instead of being a characteristic of a particular phase in the life of human beings, 'gero'transcendence might be more like a stable personality trait of some people and not (or less) of others. The same might go for spirituality in general. Atchley has suggested that with and by growing older people become more spiritual (Atchley, 2011, 2016). Perhaps it is true that many people with full-time jobs and under the pressure of a high

---

[12] See Carstensen's socioemotional selectivity theory, already discussed in Section 'Aging with Purpose'.

workload, only find the time and stimulus to stop and dwell on what they think is really important in life, when they retire. And it might be that people in Western Europe and North America were brought up more spiritually some decades ago. However, I think that spirituality can not only be found in and is not only important for older, retired people (Derkx, 2018).

MEANING IN LIFE WHILE AGING: THE WHOLE PICTURE

Up to now, the seven components of MIL have largely been treated separately, in relation to aging. I have clarified conceptually, provided results of (mostly recent) empirical research, and raised questions. However, some more general issues should be elaborated. I have selected four of these.

State, Trait, Stage, Strategy

People can experience their lives as meaningful in a particular, passing moment. Thus MIL refers to a momentary *state* of mind, to a degree of how much meaning a person reports to possess at a particular moment in time. However, this is not the only way we can interpret MIL. In the same way as subjective well-being (level of positive and negative affect and life satisfaction) (Diener et al., 2006), experiencing a certain level of MIL can perhaps be regarded as a relatively enduring personality *trait* that may change temporarily according to life circumstances but then returns to a rather stable set point for the majority of people. A third way of viewing meaning is as a mature *stage* in life which people can achieve in the development of their personality. MIL, then, is more a stage in life that can be reached, when people have, for example, found purpose in life and, reviewing their life, have learned to see coherence in it. Viewed in this developmental way, MIL is an accomplishment and not just a byproduct of objective life circumstances or lucky personal dispositions. The state-perspective easily comes forward, but it seems useful to take the trait- and stage-perspective also into account.[13] Near the very end of this text, meaning in life will be elaborated as part of a(n unconscious) *strategy*, an adaptive mechanism to deal with a hostile environment. How to combine the state, trait, stage, and strategy perspective in one theory, seems quite a challenge.

[13] Interesting publications in this respect are King and Hicks (2007) and Bauer et al. (2011).

Historical, Cultural, and Social Conditions

It is very clear that the experience of a more or less meaningful life is heavily influenced by historical, cultural, and social conditions and developments. The same goes, of course, for theories about this experience. Erik Erikson never forgot to mention the historical relativity of his psychosocial theories of the life cycle. In 1978, he wrote that his concept of the life cycle emerged "from theoretical concerns intrinsic to a historical and conceptual 'moment'" and in 1982, he added: "a look back on this century's last few decades makes it clear that *old age* was 'discovered' only in recent years (...) when an ever-increasing number of old people were found (and found themselves) to represent a mass of *elderlies* rather than an elite of *elders*" (Erikson & Erikson, 1978, p. 3; [1982] 1998, p. 12). Experiences and theories of (a meaningful) later life will also, inevitably, bear the mark of their historical moment.[14] Whether aging is experienced primarily as an existential issue or as a medical problem, is not a purely personal coincidence or choice (Cole, 1992). And earlier in this text, I already pointed to the influence of the historically contingent and changeable, socially and politically legitimized and supported average life course, for women and men (structuring when we learn, care, work, and enjoy ourselves).

A historical moment for an individual refers to his biography, but there is always a wider cultural and social context. American psychologist Ed de St. Aubin tells a story about a lunch conversation he had with Japanese scholar Yoko Yamada when both were attending a conference on generativity in 1999. Yamada said that Japanese scholars at the conference thought of the US academics present as very foolish. She explained that the Americans consistently referred to adults who score low (nongenerative) or high (generativity exemplars) on generativity. The American research enterprise seemed

> based on quantitative individual differences in generativity. For Yoko and her Japanese colleagues, this is foolish because generativity is not a phenomenon that resides within the individual. It is a collective force that exists within and between generations—moving towards us from several generations ago and moving forward to the far future. An individual adult is but a conduit through which generativity is transferred. (...) If you must examine

---

[14] Important historical studies of aging and/or gerontology are: Minois (1989), Cole (1992), Achenbaum (1995), Thane (2000), Park (2016). Cole's study is most explicit on meaning in aging.

this at the level of the individual, Yoko explained, better to question the "flavors" of one's generativity or the "colors," for there may be important *qualitative* differences in how adults manage this transaction. But no adult, in her Japanese perspective, could be thought of as more generative than another, or as less so, and certainly not as nongenerative. (de St. Aubin & Bach, 2014, p. 2)

This example is meant to emphasize that, just as research on the life cycle and on generativity, research on meaning should not only be on the lookout for historical changes but also for possible differences between (sub)cultures around the globe and within countries and societies. Individual personal positions within cultures are something else again, of course. Irish sociologist Ricca Edmondson's emphasis on individuals as basically intertwined, on communal virtues and on indirect communication (e.g., through behavior), makes me think she might have been more in agreement with the Japanese view of generativity than with the view of the (fellow Western) US scholars (Edmondson, 2015). It will be clear by now, that I am not propagating cultural difference in MIL a priori. Detailed evidence should decide. And there is evidence in diverging directions, showing, e.g., relevant differences between the US and Japan regarding self-worth and connectedness (Ryff et al., 2014) and similarities between Cameroon, the Czech Republic, Germany, and Hong Kong regarding generativity and purpose beyond the self (Hofer et al., 2014).

Historical and cultural differences are important, but within nations and cultures social class differences exist. Research by Melvin Kohn, Carmi Schooler, Paul Piff, and others has shown that, as a statistical group, people with a higher socioeconomic status or SES (measured by income, higher educational attainment, subjective social status, and/or job characteristics facilitating self-direction) show a higher self-centric orientation while manifesting lower other-orientation. Striving for one's personal goals, attempting to remain in control, and expressing and esteeming the self exemplifies a self-orientation. Caring for and helping others, adjusting to others, valuing one's social responsibility, and investing in harmonic social relations with others (connectedness) exemplify other-orientation (Miyamoto et al., 2018, pp. 428–429; see also Kohn, 1989; Schooler et al., 2004; Piff, 2014).[15] For individuals it is possible to be high on both self-orientation and other-orientation.

Recent research by Miyamoto and others has established how this psychological effect of SES can be moderated by culture. Their findings are more nuanced, but the main line is this one. In the United States, high SES and culture push in the same direction: toward self-direction. In Japan high SES pushes toward self-direction (as all over the world), but culture (also or only) toward other-direction. People with high SES are in the position to better fulfill the ideals of their culture. People with high SES in Japan were found stronger in self-directedness and in other-directedness than people with low SES. In the United States, people with high SES show stronger self-directedness but lower other-directedness (Miyamoto et al., 2018). So, if people with a higher and a lower SES both experience life as meaningful, the character of that experience (and the dimensions of meaning they emphasize) might be very different for the two groups. Carol Ryff's comment that "culture, history, ethnicity, class, and so on give rise to different, perhaps competing, conceptions of well-being" (Ryff, 1989, p. 1079), is probably not only a valid point in relation to her concept of psychological well-being but also in relation to the concept of meaning in life. For the time being, I assume that the dimensions of and needs for meaning in life discussed here are universally human. I do expect, however, that historical, cultural, and social conditions cause differences in emphasis among them and in the way dimensions are interpreted and hang together.

Balance and Compensation among Components of Meaning

Seven dimensions of meaning have been elaborated separately. But what about the set of components as a whole? One point that has to be made is that some of these components *balance* each other. But what does 'balance' mean? In the footsteps of Smaling and Alma, I have added the component connectedness, because I think Baumeister's four needs for meaning result in a picture which puts too much emphasis on agency (purpose, self-worth, autonomy, independence, control, power, dominance, achievement) and too little on communion (moral worth, love, intimacy, interdependence, responsibility, care) (Bakan, 1966; McAdams,

---

[15] I thank Dale Dannefer for drawing my attention to the publications by Kohn and Schooler.

1997; Şmaling & Alma, 2010). Agency is the motive to individuate and advance the interests of self, communion is the motive to relate to others and contribute to social cohesion. In Shalom H. Schwartz's value typology, agency conforms to the self-enhancing values of power and achievement and communion to the self-transcending values of benevolence and universalism (concern for the welfare of all) (Walker & Frimer, 2015, p. 414). In the section on moral worth, we saw that people strongly motivated by purposes beyond the self (moral purpose exemplars) do not experience these as in conflict with their personal interests; "rather, personal and moral concerns seemingly had become fused in their identity" (Walker & Frimer, 2015, p. 415). So a balance between different components of meaning for many people might be a balance between oppositional forces, but this need not be. They may also complement or strengthen each other. Self-interest may be more or less enlightened. The word 'balance' then points to the fact that for experiencing life as meaningful, both components are necessary, in a particular combination, and to a certain extent. And in the case of self-worth, control ,and connectedness, the most positive development with age does not just mean that the dimension of communion (connectedness) becomes more important, it also means that agency (self-worth, control) as a force does not disappear. Without a sense of agency, "the motivation to contribute to the greater good lacks the impetus necessary to move from judgment to action since there is little personal investment in the enterprise" (Walker & Frimer, 2015, p. 414).

Another point is that it is not clear whether the components of meaning can *compensate* each other. For example, if someone experiences a strong connection with family and/or friends, is it less necessary for this person to have a sense of purpose in order to experience life as meaningful (enough)? Is it really necessary for the experience of a meaningful life, that all seven needs for meaning are adequately satisfied? And, of course, the experience of life as meaningful need not be a yes or no question. In extreme cases, it might be, but often it will be a matter of degree: Life is experienced as meaningful, but to a lower or higher degree.

Hong Zhang et al. recently reported on one example of compensation among sources of MIL.[16] They investigated whether individuals reduce the importance attached to social relationships for MIL and turn to

---

[16] Zhang and colleagues write about meaning in life in an undifferentiated, general way and then distinguish between many different *sources* of meaning such as belongingness (social relationships) and self-esteem. My theory of meaning in life distinguishes between seven different needs for meaning as defining components or dimensions of meaning in life. Many sources can contribute to the fulfilment of these needs.

alternative sources of meaning when the need to belong (the need for this important type of connectedness) is frustrated. The research involved 3 related studies with each about 100 undergraduate and graduate students (ages ranged from 17 to 39) from Nanjing University, China. Study 1 and especially study 2 are very relevant here. Study 1 showed that those who had a stronger sense of belonging (measured by the response to five items such as 'I feel like there are many people with whom I belong') were more likely to believe that social relationships made their lives meaningful (measured by the response to two questions like 'What makes your life meaningful?') and to possess higher levels of MIL (measured by the response to five items such as 'I understand my life's meaning'). In experimental study 2, participants were randomly divided into three groups and the members of these groups were manipulated by having them write about two people to whom they felt they belonged (the belongingness group), about two people who left them with the feelings of being rejected, excluded, or ignored (the exclusion group) or about two people with whom they had recently interacted (the control group). After completing this task, participants filled out questionnaires measuring their sense of belonging, presence of MIL, and perceived importance of four potential sources of MIL: social relationships, autonomy, personal goals, and social commitment. Autonomy, for example, was measured by the response to four items such as 'I feel meaningless when I have to act against my own will.' The results showed that priming participants with social exclusion successfully reduced individuals' sense of belonging. The results also demonstrated a clear case of compensation. The three experimental groups differed significantly in the degrees of basing MIL on social relationships and autonomy, but not in the other two sources of meaning; personal goals and social commitment.

> [C]ompared to participants in the belonging and control groups, those in the exclusion group were less likely to base their MIL on social relationships (…), but more likely to base MIL on autonomy (…). However, participants in the belonging and control conditions did not report any significant difference in how much they based MIL on any of the sources. (…) Our results showed that participants whose belongingness was threatened by reminders of social exclusion attempted to reaffirm their MIL through an alternative source (i.e. autonomy) (…) However, this endeavour did not seem to be successful as participants in the exclusion condition reported lower levels of MIL compared to those in the other two groups. Therefore, the vital role of social relationships in meaning-making does not appear to be easily substituted. (Zhang et al., 2019, p. 247)

Interestingly, the compensation process turned out to be selective. As an alternative for (threatened) belongingness, participants did not opt for an increased reliance on personal goals or social commitment. Perhaps they chose autonomy as a promising alternative because autonomy is in some ways antagonistic to belongingness. This raises the issue whether, speaking more broadly, agency and communion might be able to compensate for each other in some way. In light of the above, communion might be more difficult to compensate for than agency. However, this is all very tentative speculation. As Zhang and colleagues write: "the substitutability among sources of MIL is an interesting yet complicated question" (2019, p. 252). And it is another question again whether compensation works differently for older people, in comparison to the adolescent and young adult participants Zhang et al. worked with.

The issue of compensation is more important because in dealing with the separate components, we saw with each and all of them that they overlap, influence, or co-determine one or more of the other components. Perhaps factor analysis (see the reference to Morgan and Farsides at the beginning of Section 'On Excitement') could also be used to get more insight into the relationships between the different components/dimensions of meaning distinguished here. In this way perhaps, we can see whether really all of them are necessary to get a clear picture of what makes human lives meaningful.

Meaning in Life and Well-Being

The last more general issue I will deal with in this chapter is the relationship between MIL and well-being. To enable a decent discussion of this issue, it is important to say something about terminology. Two important traditions in well-being research have to be distinguished: Ed Diener's 'subjective well-being' and Carol Ryff's 'psychological well-being.' The terminology is a bit confusing. Subjective well-being is also a 'psychological' concept. And although psychological well-being starts from six dimensions, psychological theory has established as objectively important for human beings (Tiberius, 2015, p. 176), the scores on these dimensions are also 'subjective' ratings by research participants. Subjective well-being (SWB) is intentionally theory-meagre. With the SWB approach, researchers want the respondents in their surveys to decide for themselves what they think important for their well-being. SWB is often called 'hedonic' well-being and mainly refers to the frequency of short-term (a moment, a day, or a week) positive and negative affect and to a longer-term (e.g., a month or a year) cognitive evaluation of life, i.e., life satisfaction. Positive and negative affect often are experienced simultaneously.

> The findings, in general, indicate that effects of life stories on the SWB of older people combine memories of both happiness and suffering in those stories. (...) For example, a participant told of how he frightfully watched his house ruined in war, and yet felt happy about remaining in life; another participant told about the joy she had of having all her grandchildren united with her in a family celebration, yet acutely feeling the pain that her husband had not survived to that moment. (Shmotkin, 2011, p. 39)

Research has shown that most people sustain an above-medium, positive baseline of SWB and that people after a while tend to adapt back to their SWB baseline following adversity as well as lucky events. Research also established that the level of positive affect is relatively independent from that of negative affect. And it shows that SWB does not necessarily decrease with advancing age (Diener & Diener, 1996; Mroczek & Kolarz, 1998; Shmotkin & Shrira, 2012, pp. 144–145).

Psychological well-being (PWB) is often called 'eudaimonic' well-being and refers to six dimensions of well-being distilled from important psychological theories about personality and human development, about optimal actualization of one's talents, and about facing existential life challenges. The six dimensions are: purpose in life, environmental mastery, positive relationships, personal growth, autonomy, and self-acceptance. As with SWB, people seem to sustain a personal baseline of PWB. Longitudinal profiles of PWB "reveal notable stability over a 9- to 10-year period— some are persistently high in their levels of eudaimonic well-being across time, while others are persistently low" (Ryff, 2017, p. 166). In the representative US national sample of the MIDUS study (aged 25–74), some aspects of PWB (e.g., environmental mastery, autonomy) show increments with age, others show decrements (e.g., purpose in life, personal growth), and others show little variation with age (self-acceptance). For positive relations with others, patterns have varied between showing stable or incremental age profiles. These patterns could reflect age changes or cohort differences (or both) (Ryff et al., 2004, pp. 399, 416–417). These patterns also show that it is important to have a multidimensional concept of well-being, because life-course trajectories can show gains in some areas, and losses or stability in other ones. To only use an overall measure, would hide a lot.

Factor analyses by Keyes, Shmotkin, and Ryff (using a representative US sample of 3032 respondents who were interviewed for 45 minutes on average and who completed 2 questionnaire booklets) confirmed that SWB and PWB are related and partly overlapping concepts, but also that they are distinct and unique facets of a more general well-being. Purpose in life and personal growth are the PWB dimensions that most clearly separate PWB from SWB. Having high SWB with low PWB is typical of older adults with lower education. Having low SWB with high PWB is typical of younger adults with higher education. High SWB and high PWB combined has been called 'optimal well-being.' The probability to register optimal well-being increases as age, education, extraversion, and conscientiousness increase and as neuroticism decreases (Keyes et al., 2002).[17]

It is confusing that authors sometimes refer to SWB as 'happiness' and 'quality of life' and to PWB as 'meaning,' 'thriving,' or 'flourishing.' It is true that the six dimensions of PWB show considerable overlap with our seven dimensions of MIL, but differences also remain. Is autonomy the same as a combination of self-worth, moral worth, control, and coherence? Coherence is at least not completely the same as self-acceptance (what about world-acceptance?). And moral worth is an important part of MIL that seems to be absent in psychological well-being.[18] SWB, PWB, and MIL can all be regarded as concepts expressing a way in which life can be good (or bad), but differences between the three approaches clearly remain.

Baumeister and colleagues have conducted an exploratory study on the distinction between a happy life and a meaningful life (Baumeister et al., 2013). They regard meaningfulness as "both a cognitive and an emotional assessment of whether one's life has purpose and value." And although they assume that there is considerable overlap between happiness and

---

[17] Other important and instructive publications on (the distinction between) 'subjective' (hedonic) and 'psychological' (eudaimonic) well-being are: Ryan and Deci (2001), Diener et al. (2009), Ryff (2014).

[18] Apart from SWB and PWB, the two dominant conceptions of well-being, Corey Keyes has argued that 'individuals remain embedded in social structures and communities, and face countless social tasks and challenges. To understand optimal functioning and mental health, social scientists also should investigate adults' social well-being' (Keyes, 1998, p. 122). For reasons of space, I cannot go into this here; see also Keyes and Shapiro (2004).

meaningfulness, they also assume "it should be possible to have a highly meaningful life that is not necessarily a happy one (e.g. as religious missionary, political activist, or terrorist)" (both quotes are from Baumeister et al., 2013, p. 506). Baumeister and colleagues' main source of data for the difference between happiness and meaningfulness were three consecutive surveys completed by a US national sample of 397 adults (68% female; ages 18–78; M = 35,5 years old; 48.1% were parents). The second survey was completed 1 week after the first one, and the final survey was completed 3 weeks after the second one. Happiness and meaningfulness were measured by the agreeing/disagreeing responses on a 1–7 scale to parallel statements in which the word 'happy' (3 statements) or 'meaningful' (also 3 statements) occurred. Examples of the statements are: "In general I consider myself happy" and "Compared to most of my peers, my life is meaningful." This means that the roughly 400 participants defined happiness (hedonic or eudaimonic or?) and a meaningful life (according to the will of God, purposeful, or?) in whatever way they chose. Participants also answered questions on a large number of other variables happiness and/or meaning might be correlated with. In the analysis and discussion of the results, the researchers defined happiness as a balance between positive and negative affect (a central part of SWB).[19] Happiness and meaningfulness turned out to have considerable overlap and to be substantially and positively correlated. Baumeister et al. explicitly do not deny or ignore this and that is important,[20] but in this study they were looking for variables that correlated positively with happiness but negatively with meaningfulness, and vice versa. They were looking for the difference between the two concepts. At the end of their article they give 'a statistical portrait' of a life that is highly meaningful but relatively low in happiness and of a highly

---

[19] Baumeister et al. (2013, p. 515): 'The current discussion of what happiness feels like, does, and means, therefore, does not capture the kind of happiness that is eud[ai]monia because we statistically separated levels of positive feelings (our definition of happiness) from a sense of meaning.'

[20] So they do not have to disagree with the findings of Anne Colby et al. and Hanne Laceulle which I mention in Section 'Moral Worth and Aging'. According to Colby et al. empirical research shows that people who are strongly committed to the common good do not seem to sacrifice self-oriented pursuits. They treat engaging beyond the self as entirely compatible with doing fun and interesting things and seeking personal growth. According to Laceulle's philosophical argument the purpose to be realized in self-realization includes the ability to engage with the good of others, and through this engagement to realize our own fulfilment.

happy but relatively meaningless life. The unhappy but meaningful life is described as more cultural and uniquely human:

> [It is] seriously involved in difficult undertakings and marked by ample worry, stress, argument, and anxiety. People with such lives spend much time thinking about past and future: They expect to do a lot of deep thinking, they imagine future events, and they reflect on past struggles and challenges. They perceive themselves as having had more unpleasant experiences than others (…) High meaningfulness despite low happiness was associated with being a giver rather than a taker. These people were likely to say that taking care of children reflected them, as did buying gifts for others. Such people may self-regulate well, as indicated by their reflecting on past struggles and imagining the future, and also in their tendency to reward themselves. (Baumeister et al., 2013, p. 515)

The highly happy but relatively meaningless life is depicted as more natural, biological, more a matter of satisfying needs and wants.

> People with such lives seem rather carefree, lacking in worries and anxieties. If they argue, they do not feel that arguing reflects them. Interpersonally, they are takers rather than givers, and they devote little thought to past and future. These patterns suggest that happiness without meaning characterizes a relatively shallow, self-absorbed or even selfish life, in which things go well, needs and desires are easily satisfied, and difficult or taxing entanglements are avoided. (Baumeister et al., 2013, p. 515)

Baumeister et al. present the striving for happiness as something in which humans resemble other animals (perhaps with some added complexity) and the quest for meaning as a uniquely human feature. It is worth noting further that positive relationships with other persons (connectedness) are important for both the happy and the meaningful person, but in different ways. The happy person profits from other people, the person with a meaningful life cares for them. So, although a happy and a meaningful life show considerable overlap and are substantially and positively correlated, they have different emphases and can be distinguished. Especially the dimensions of moral worth and coherence, I suggest, make that it is more adequate to view humanism and religions as frames of reference for meaning and not for happiness.

Another interesting perspective on the relation between well-being and meaning is formulated in three articles/chapters on the relation between

SWB and MIL by Dov Shmotkin, Amit Shrira, and other Israeli researchers. The texts appeared in 2011–2013 (Shrira et al., 2011; Shmotkin & Shrira, 2012, 2013). It is important to point out immediately that the authors use data on MIL that are collected using several different operational definitions of MIL. Sometimes they even equate MIL with PWB (eudaimonic well-being) (Shmotkin & Shrira, 2013, p. 81). So Shmotkin and Shrira's publications on SWB and MIL sometimes actually are about SWB and PWB. As indicated, PWB does indeed have more overlap with MIL than SWB. PWB, however, is not the same as MIL. We should be aware of this, but still the texts by Shmotkin and colleagues offer relevant material and suggestions about the relation between well-being and meaning. The core of Shmotkin and Shrira's view is that SWB and MIL are not regarded, as is usual in psychology, as end *results* or *outcomes* of ways of life, psychological dispositions, life events, biographies, sociodemographic characteristics, social environments et cetera, but as *means*, adaptive mechanisms, *strategies*, 'agentic forces,' or 'dynamic systems' to deal with living in a world that at any moment can turn out to be hostile (or more hostile if it is already). So MIL cannot only be viewed as state, trait, and stage, but also as (unconscious) strategy. The hostile-world-scenario (HWS) represents life-adversity and is a personal image of actual or potential threats to one's life or, more broadly, to one's physical and mental integrity (e.g., natural disaster, war, bereavement, violence, crime, family breakups, poverty, accidents, illness, risk of death). The HWS can be activated adaptively and then it helps to remain vigilant and prudent in the struggle to remain safe and well. An extreme HWS, however, can generate a continuous sense of survivorship in a disastrous world and obstruct adaptation. In this context, SWB and MIL provide distinct, yet complementary functions of regulation and reconstruction. SWB regulates in the sense that it makes adversity more manageable by letting individuals evaluate their lives positively even in negative conditions. MIL reconstructs in the sense that it makes adversity more interpretable by letting individuals conceive their lives in comprehensible terms.

> Put otherwise, SWB *regulates* the activation of HWS whereas MIL *reconstructs* its contents. (…) Thus, by regulating the HWS, SWB constitutes a favourable psychological environment that facilitates the generation and awareness of MIL (…) In parallel, a meaningful reconstruction of the HWS facilitates resilient self-perceptions and beneficial engagements that may summon a stronger SWB. (Shmotkin & Shrira, 2013, p. 79)

Besides having their own unique and separate functions, SWB and MIL interact and have two complementary functions. When life adversity intensifies in terms of a stronger HWS or in terms of the actual occurrence of terrifying events, SWB and MIL *amplify* each other and get more closely associated. For example, the association between positive affect and MIL increases when loneliness is high and satisfaction from social relationships is low, and also when the perception of future time becomes limited. The amplification may be explained by the increasing need, when adversity becomes intense, to mobilize resources residing in the overlap between SWB and MIL (Shmotkin & Shrira, 2013, p. 80).[21] The second complementary function occurs when adversity becomes stronger and one construct is low (either SWB or MIL). The other construct then *compensates* for that, and protects functioning. For example, "when MIL is gravely undermined by adversity, SWB becomes more tightly associated with functioning, as even the smallest amount of satisfaction or happiness may be cardinal to replenish one's coping strengths" (Shmotkin & Shrira, 2013, p. 80).[22]

The findings above derive from a variable-centered approach, seeking to explain relations between variables across their full distributions in a whole sample. Shmotkin and Shrira also present results from a person-centered approach, which classifies individuals into subgroups within the investigated sample according to their differential standing on the variables of interest. This can be done in a more or less-detailed manner. In a more general manner, one can, e.g., distinguish a subgroup of people with low SWB and high MIL (unhappy persons who lead noble lives) from a subgroup with high SWB and low MIL (Baumeister et al's highly happy persons with a relatively meaningless life) and study and compare these groups. Shmotkin and Shrira suggest that the common appealing image of people with high SWB and low MIL is illusory. Their happiness is based in an unrealistic perception of life and, as such, it will be less resilient in the face of life's difficulties than the bittersweet happiness of the people integrating the recognition of loss and the fragility of human intention (see also King & Hicks, 2007, p. 633). Bauer, Schwab, and McAdams have a different interpretation of more or less the same configuration. They write

---

[21] Here Shmotkin and Shrira refer to research by Joshua Hicks et al. published in 2010 and 2012.
[22] Here Shmotkin and Shrira refer to research by Barbara Fredrickson et al. published in 2003.

about persons with high SWB and low MIL as people who are dispositionally happy, e.g., by winning the genetical or environmental lottery. These persons travel, in the words of Bauer et al., the short road to well-being. People who are not happy by disposition and who do not gloss over life's difficulties, have the possibility of working hard at the development of their ego, at ego-integrity (integrating human suffering and inequities), coherence, and acceptance of the way things are. Ego-integrity generally does not emerge before midlife. Coherence is not only a component of a static sense of MIL; it can also be viewed as an achievement, as a stage in personal development. This is the long road to well-being. People traveling this road are not happy from the start, but finally, when they achieve ego-integrity, happiness increases remarkably (Bauer et al., 2011, pp. 130–132).

A more detailed way of classifying people into subgroups is used, e.g., when people with high positive affect (component of SWB) and high purpose in life (component of PWB and MIL) are compared with the subgroup with high positive personal relations (component of PWB and MIL) and low purpose in life. In this way many concurrent combinations (configurations or profiles) of individuals' positions across different SWB and MIL dimensions can be studied as a more or less successful unconscious strategy used by a subgroup of people who strive to optimize their perceived lives and/or to ward off the threats facing them in a hostile world (Shmotkin & Shrira, 2013).

Concluding Remarks and Discussion

At the end of this text in which many aspects of and perspectives on meaning in life have been treated, I will only add a few very important points, for emphasis and discussion. The first discussion point is that recently I have started to wonder whether a theory of MIL cannot do without the component of self-worth. Let me explain.

1. Indications exist that a large part of self-esteem is covered by moral worth. See, for example, the 14 items of the 'self-esteem' scale devised by Viktor Gecas and Michael L. Schwalbe (referred to in 1990, p. 168). The 14 items (on the positive pole) are: powerful, honest, good, confident, kind, strong, dependable, wise, do things well, brave, generous, attractive, tolerant, and worthy. Several of them could also be part of a 'moral worth' scale.

2. Baumeister published his book *Meanings of Life* in 1991. In that book, he promotes a sense of high self-esteem as a component of the experience of a meaningful life. In 1996, Baumeister et al. published an article on the dark side of self-esteem, showing a link with violence and aggression. Looking back in 2018, he writes that "he had initially been a strong proponent of the importance of self-esteem but had gradually converted into a skeptic" (Baumeister & Vohs, 2018, p. 138). This same article ends with the remark that "at present, we would speculate that schools, organizations, and society at large would benefit more by cultivating self-control than self-esteem." This development in Baumeister's judgment contributes to my doubts about self-worth as a necessary component of MIL, given the fact that both moral worth and control already are such components.
3. Perhaps it is better to view self-worth as a component of happiness and moral worth as a component of meaningfulness (Ronkes Agerbeek, 2016, pp. 37–40, 66–67). Ironically, again it is Baumeister himself who provides an important part of the argument. As we just saw, Baumeister et al. in 2013 published an article on the difference between a happy life and a meaningful life. One of the conclusions of this article does not say so, but it almost reads like an argument for regarding self-worth as part of happiness and moral worth as part of meaningfulness. The conclusion of the authors is:

> Our findings suggest that happiness is mainly about getting what one wants and needs, including from other people or even just by using money. In contrast, meaningfulness was linked to doing things that express and reflect the self and in particular to doing positive things for others. Meaningful involvements increase one's stress, worries, arguments, and anxiety, which reduce happiness. (…) Happiness went with being a taker more than a giver, while meaningfulness was associated with being a giver more than a taker. Whereas happiness was focused on feeling good in the present, meaningfulness integrated past, present, and future, and it sometimes meant feeling bad. (Baumeister et al., 2013, p. 515)[23]

---

[23] In Crescioni and Baumeister (2013, p. 7), the meaning need for self-worth almost reads as the need for connectedness. Via 'the esteem with which one is regarded by others', self-worth is interpreted as 'belongingness' and as the opposite of 'chronic loneliness' and 'social rejection'.

4. Finally, by examining Japanese culture Heine et al. have argued that the need for positive self-regard is not a universal, but is rooted in significant aspects of Western, specifically North American culture (Heine et al., 1999).

So, maybe, we should revise our theory of a meaningful life and drop 'self-worth' as a defining component of MIL. This does not imply that the experience of a meaningful life generally conflicts with a sense of self-worth, but only that the six remaining components together better cover the semantic core of meaningfulness than the set of seven components including self-worth.

The seven (or six) dimensions of MIL can balance and compensate each other. How exactly is a very complicated issue. A balance between different components of meaning may be a balance between oppositional forces, but this need not be. They may also complement or strengthen each other. In the case of self-worth, control, and connectedness, the better development with age does not just mean that the dimension of connectedness becomes more important, it also means that agency (self-worth, control) as a force does not disappear. Without a sense of agency, the motivation to contribute to the greater good seldom moves from judgment to action. MIL can be regarded as one way to view well-being or the good life, besides approaches such as SWB and PWB. Most often researchers regard MIL as a favorable psychological state, but sometimes as a personality trait, as a developmental stage, or as an adaptive strategy confronting a (possibly) hostile environment. I have discussed all of this in the preceding section.

The component of MIL most often regarded as a developmental achievement is *coherence* (ego-integrity). Coherence is more about being able, cognitively and emotionally, to accept one's life as a whole, than about finding complete and ever-lasting intellectual unity and consistency in one's life story. *Purpose* is the component of MIL which is most uncontroversial. All views and measures of MIL incorporate a purpose dimension. As people age, the sense of purpose seems to decrease, but, at least as important, it also seems to change in character. Some authors think that especially coherence (ego-integrity) goals grow in importance with age, others think that emotional meaningfulness goals become more salient. One of the ways people use to get or keep a sense of *control* is to de-emphasize the importance of goals that have become difficult to achieve and to focus instead on more reachable goals. Perceived control in the

German population increased until ages 30–40, then decreased until approximately age 60, and increased more or less slightly afterwards. In the United States, the trajectory of perceived control is very similar, with one remarkable difference. For Americans over 60 perceived control declined at an accelerated rate down to an extremely low level. The explanation of the difference points to better retirement funding in Germany. This is only one of many, many instances in which (a component of) meaning in life is co-determined by *historical, cultural, and/or social conditions*. *Self-worth* overlaps with control and moral worth. I have argued that it is perhaps better to drop self-worth as a defining component of MIL. *Excitement* is a component of MIL, which is hard to pin down and depends very much on the details of a person's life narrative. When people are asked to select *the* special meaningful moment in their life, some people mention routine, even daily moments. These people see something very extraordinary in something usual and ordinary. *Connectedness* in the sense of positive personal relationships (family, friends) is a very important defining element or source of MIL, also or especially for older people. Connectedness in the sense of feeling part of something larger than a group of close personal relations is also important. Generativity and gerotranscendence are examples of this more spiritual type of connectedness. When first formulated, these two phenomena were linked to a particular stage in personal development, midlife and old age respectively, but research has shown that they are more like rather stable personality traits, that, however, can be fostered.

Discussions about generativity and gerotranscendence have a moral dimension (wanting to contribute to and feeling responsible for future generations) as do most discussions about what makes life meaningful. Narcissism can provide life with meaning, but it is not to be applauded. And, however regrettable, horrible ideas and purposes, such as those of the Nazi regime, can contribute to a strong sense of meaning in life. The most distinctive component of MIL is a sense of *moral worth*. This dimension has received little attention in gerontology as well as in psychological approaches to well-being. It must be admitted that it is difficult to reach rational consensus about the best answer to important ethical and political questions. In practice, however, decisions will be taken, one way or the other. So rather than evade these questions, it is better to engage in public debates about them and offer arguments, reasons, and considerations as best as we can. Knowledge of history and philosophy are useful here. In its choice of problems to tackle, science should prioritize the most important problems and not the problems that can be dealt with by the easiest methods or the methods that lead to the most firm and unshakable results. As Karl Popper already argued in 1958, we should not dualistically, in the way of nineteenth-century positivism, distinguish between scientific and nonsensical approaches to problems. Three approaches have to be distinguished: (1) the way of rational empirical science in which descriptions, explanations, and predictions can be falsified or corroborated if not proven, (2) the approach of rational science in a wider sense (including philosophy) in which existential, religious, ontological, ethical, and political issues are the subject of debates in which reasons and considerations are exchanged (but empirical falsification or proof is impossible), and (3) the irrational approach in which authority, force, prejudice, deceit, or something similar is decisive (Popper, [1958] 1989). In gerontological circles, the dualistic view of science, in a very strict and limiting sense versus no reason at all, still seems to dominate. Ricca Edmondson ends her explanation of this situation with the remark: "In the realm of gerontology, the preference for eschewing debates about values is enough to make it hard to discuss lifetime meaning at all" (Edmondson, 2015, p. 10). Life-span developmental psychologist Anne Colby says it this way:

> When new students arrive to work with my colleagues and me at the Stanford Graduate School of Education, I often share with them an article called "Virtue Development and Psychology's Fear of Normativity," by the philosopher Kristján Kristjánsson (2012). The paper argues that psychologists can benefit from collaborating with philosophers since it is impossible to avoid taking values positions, and justifications of those positions are conceptual and philosophical rather than solely empirical. Moral psychology, even more than other fields, entails normative or prescriptive questions—about what it means to be morally mature, and about what kinds of moral responses are of higher quality and ought to be supported and nurtured. After all, the field of moral psychology is important partly because we want to understand what contributes to positive morality—honesty, fairness, compassion, respect, and the like—so we can encourage it. Conversely, we need to understand negative moral behavior—cruelty, injustice, corruption—in order to prevent and discourage it. The distinctions at the heart of this work are not, at base, empirical issues. They require statements of value—moral commitments. (Colby et al., 2020, pp. 1–2)

Colby's observations not only pertain to the study of how to educate young people. The study of meaningful aging inevitably involves normative or prescriptive questions. What is the best way to politically organize the life course? Around "work as the be-all and end-all of life"? (Edmondson, 2015, p. 15). When research shows that older adults often are found to have a higher SWB than younger ones, but a lower sense of purpose, is that a result to celebrate or to worry about? And when Shalom H. Schwartz and colleagues, for another example, discovered that a higher age correlated positively with regarding certain values as more important (see Section 'Moral Worth and Aging'), what normative conclusions can we/should we draw in the light of this empirical finding? Social scientists often are afraid to take a position on moral issues in their publications, even if their descriptions and explanations almost demand it.[24] They seem to think that taking sides will harm their position as an independent expert, but they forget that objective analysis of situations and developments can practically ask for partisanship. Refusing to become engaged for the good cause harms one's status as a reliable human being. Moral and social philosophers are trained in arguing for and against normative positions and in developing theories about the good life and the good society, but they often lack detailed empirical knowledge. Part of what is urgently needed for progress in (the study of) meaningful living and aging is *interdisciplinary collaboration* between social scientists, historians, and philosophers. This is a complex undertaking, but it is sorely needed. Where there's a will there's a way.

---

[24] There are more exceptions, of course, than Anne Colby. She herself refers to William Damon. And Carol Ryff published an article with a section called "Understanding the sources and broader consequences of greed at the top" (Ryff, 2017, pp. 170–172).

CHAPTER 3

The Longevity of Justice: Assessing Peter Derkx's Approach

Abstract Derkx defines humanism as a "meaning frame"—i.e., cultural coding serving to map out movement toward a positive identity and a stable existence—by means of which life is given value and significance. Meaningful life has something to do with healthy relationships that nurture and provide a way to address the nature of existence through a balance between what one is and what one does. This, of course, assumes the ability to develop arrangements that presume the basic goodness of humanity as the ability to distinguish "negative freedom" and "positive freedom," and act accordingly. Mindful of this general discussion, this chapter explores Derkx's thinking on meaningful life in relationship to current struggles for social justice and raises a question: What does it mean to seek practices of aging well as a primary humanist value? What are the consequences for aging well when humans are positioned within a context of racial and gender violence? The chapter concludes that, while Derkx rightly calls for addressing injustice as part of his work on life meaning, there are gaps in his aging-well logic based on certain optimistic assumptions concerning the human's ability to transform social arrangements.

Keywords Justice • Racism • Gender bias • Meaning frame • Technology

Introduction

What is it to live with meaning, to live well, and what might humanism contribute to human wrestling with such questions? Such questions are of central concern to a host of scholars, and numerous institutions have given them a central place within their research agendas. For example, aging well has been a major intellectual project at the University of Humanistic Studies (Utrecht). And numerous articles and books have developed as members of that University's faculty think through the ramifications of this duality of being—resilience and aging. A key figure within this discussion has been Peter Derkx, and it is to his work that I turn my attention in this chapter (Derkx, 2009, 2013a, 2013b).

I am particularly interested in Derkx's work related to the dynamics of aging well as played out within the social framework of a humanist worldview. But I mean to think through his position on this issue in relationship to issues of social justice, and I do so through a close and critical read of three of his English language publications on life extension. Furthermore, I bring Derkx's interests and mine together by exploring resilience and aging through attention to people whose social meaning and the nature of their aging are negatively affected by racism and gender bias. Hence, the question of this chapter: Considering struggles for social justice, what does it mean to seek practices of aging well as a primary humanist value?

I begin by reviewing, while offering some commentary on, a few of Derkx's major assertions. This preliminary work is followed by a series of observations meant to think through the applicability of his assertions within a context prioritizing issues of social justice as opposed to a context assuming a more generally framed humanity as the subject of quality of life enhancement. In this way, one might note, I aim to think through Derkx's ideas in light of the realities of embodied bodies living in a context of social possibilities and restrictions arranged in light of socio-cultural markers of meaning such as race and gender.

On Humanism and Humanist Values

"Meaning frame." With these two words Derkx summarizes his understanding of the nature and meaning of humanism and, he argues, it is synergistically connected to what we intend when speaking of a "meaningful life" (Derkx, 2013a, p. 42). This being the case, and drawing from a variety of thinkers, Derkx argues a meaningful life involves connections, or a network of relationships that enhance existence and offer substantive responses to the fundamental questions of human existence (the metaphysical challenges that define, to a certain extent, human history). Hence, it, a meaningful life, has something to do with recognition and acceptance of the weight of one's existence in such a way as to produce harmony between what one is and what one does. A meaningful life involves layered, complex, and tangled significance in connection to others and the world, which, by extension, produces mental and physical health benefits (Derkx, 2013a, pp. 43–4, 48).

These connections (e.g., people to each other and to the world) are intended as positive, transformative, and vital to well-being. Without this sense, say, of movement beyond the self, according to Derkx, life "would contain too much agency and too little communion. Dependency, attachment, wonder, vulnerability and care are important aspects of life and the need for connectedness, and transcendence does justice to them" (Derkx, 2013a, p. 47). In short, this sense of "meaningful life" involves at least seven components of contact—"the need for purpose, moral worth, self-worth, competence, comprehensibility, connectedness, and transcendence" (Derkx, 2013a, p. 47). These seven components of meaning are also elaborated by Derkx, where transcendence is replaced by excitement. As a point of clarification, a distinction, he argues, must be made between meaning and happiness. The former involves the seven components harnessed together in such a way that they come to constitute a particular cartography of human existence that proposes the outline of meaning (Derkx, 2013a, p. 48). Happiness, on the other hand, is a secondary impulse or motivation in that the quest for meaning can drive life without happiness.

Having explored and unpacked the nature of *life* meaning, Derkx turns his attention to meaning *frames*, noting that they constitute a map of sorts, or mechanisms for determining one's push toward "direction, stability, identity, and continuity" (Derkx, 2013a, p. 49). There is something social about these frames in that they are passed on typically through networks in which and by means of which humans are socialized or introduced to the cultural arrangements of life (Derkx, 2013a, p. 49). Still, there is no single set of frames used by all; rather, each person and each community formulate frames or mechanisms for assessing and directing meaning vis-à-vis interrogation of experience for what it says about the large and fundamental concerns of existence. Humanism, he concludes, is one of these contextually understood frames.

When outlining the inner workings of humanism (i.e., the inherent principles shaping it), Derkx begins with the notion that humanism is contextually bound as it is not a *sui generis* "something" but rather it is an element of human culture concerned with the epistemological and ontological dimensions of human existence (Derkx, 2013a, p. 49). In other words, the first principle of humanism captures humans as responsive to metaphysical concerns through reflexivity and a vulnerable engagement with the world. Yet, this is not a traditional, theistic metaphysics; rather, it is historically situated and experientially grounded, and it is already and always empirically explored and known. This metaphysics influences our understanding and movement, but it is also informed by our thinking and doing. Related to this doing, Derkx argues for a common moral principle as the second tenant of humanism: People should be treated with dignity and as equals without restrictions based on socio-cultural constructions such as race and gender (Derkx, 2013a, p. 51).

There is something deeply individualistic about this principle, and therefore consistent with a dominant Western take on humanism, in that Derkx wants to maintain an understanding of the individual as best equipped to determine the parameters of his or her life, while always mindful of the right of others to do likewise. There is something about this that harkens back to early definitions of humanism—the "human as the measure of all things" (e.g., Lamont, Corliss 1997). This isn't to blame Derkx for being 'Western' in this sense, but rather to point out an ongoing assumption concerning the somewhat autonomous nature of the individual within Western thought. Yet how does one avoid radical individualism that loses quickly any regard for the significance of communal obligation and identity? Tied to this individualism are certain assumptions regarding the inevitability of human progress based on the values of reason and logic, and buttressed by scientific advances. There is a robust claim to growth and the maturation of the human race drawn from the sciences over against the more pessimistic anthropology found in numerous religious traditions. And, while much of what has constituted Enlightenment optimism and theories of progress have been critiqued and deconstructed in recent years, there are still ways in which certain strands of humanist thought still house it. Hints of Enlightenment optimism, for instance, seem to surface in what Derkx argues regarding the inner workings of humanism such as:

1. An ontology marked by the general goodness of people when given an opportunity to do the good.
2. The ability of humans to recognize and know the good.
3. The assumption logic and reason can decipher the framework of human interactions.
4. A somewhat disembodied sense of the human.
5. The human proclivity toward advancement and technological growth (Derkx, 2013a, pp. 51–57)

Still, it is important to note the Enlightenment has an unpleasant underbelly—marked by an epistemology that assumes the irrelevance of non-Europeans; the use of technology to hamper life options for 'outsider' groups such as the mechanisms of colonialism that framed the relationship of many European countries to other areas of the world, and so on. How, the question should be asked, should a discourse on longevity reflect a measured sense of optimism linked to a deep recognition of the great potential for harm?

By exploring both negative freedom (what should not occur) and positive freedom (what should be done), Derkx seeks to at least implicitly address the question I propose above. The former, negative freedom, is captured in the first two principles that privilege the good—with the assumption, it seems, that the good as perceived by the individual will have benefits for the whole, the larger community.[11] The latter, positive freedom, he suggests can constitute another principle of humanism that works in concert with the first, two core principles discussed earlier. It is concerned with making decisions and acting in the world in ways that enhance one's life and, by extension, improve life options for others. Yet, I would caution this mutual benefit isn't necessarily the case—if one

---

[1] What I offer here in terms of freedom is different from what is noted by negative and positive freedom for figures such as Isaiah Berlin. However, my aim in this essay is to situate more prominently marginalized communities. In Berlin's analysis of freedom marginalized communities—e.g., African Americans—do not figure in a significant way. For, for instance, Isaiah Berlin, "Two Concepts of Liberty," in David Miller, editor. *Liberty* (Oxford: Oxford University Press, 1991), 33–57. Anthony Fiscella's dissertation provides an important corrective to Western notions of freedom that are individualistic in nature and that exclude the manner in which 'freedom' is premised on the 'unfreedom' of certain populations. See, Fiscella, Universal Burdens: Stories of (Un)Freedom from the Unitarian Universalist Association, The MOVE Organization, and Taqwacore (Center for Theology and Religious Studies (Lund University—Lund, Sweden, 2015).

understands that oppression is web-like in nature. That is to say, while Derkx doesn't seem to move in this direction, oppression has benefits for some. And so, isn't it conceivable that this third principle could re-enforce certain modalities of oppression rather than reduce them—if one maintains the individual's well-being as the measure of humanistic success? Furthermore, what of the external influences, barriers, and mechanisms that impinge upon the individual and thereby serve to shape opportunities and limitations? Can one really safely assume the individual maneuvers through the world without being informed by external forces? Is the individual really insulated from such external mechanisms of conduct determination?

Derkx, to the extent he mentions injustice such as racism and gender-bias can't believe such socially constructed and culturally, politically, and economically operating devices don't affect and influence individuals. However, how does this realization play-out in the shaping of the various principles of humanism? Derkx provides a corrective when arguing, "the social is not a later and secondary addition to the individual" (Derkx, 2013a, p. 53). Rather, it is best to think of the individual within the context of community—the individual always and already in relationship to others and the world, and the well-being of all as the final objective and the ultimate measure of ethical and moral insight (Derkx, 2013a: 54). It is this thinking that, for Derkx, constitutes a fourth principle of humanism—when acted out not with respect to abstract humans in general, but with regard to actual, concrete people moving through time and space (Derkx, 2013a, p. 54). Derkx concludes his definition of humanism via meaning frames with attention to what he calls normative principles—"human dignity, self-fulfillment, and love of unique, irreplaceable human beings…" (Derkx, 2013a, p. 55). The test of these principles when taken as a unit involves quality of life in the form of longevity. By this, Derkx doesn't mean anything related to immortality, but rather longevity has to do with the acceptance of eventual demise within the context of long years of vital and vibrant living in relationship with and to others.

Connected to this thinking, of necessity, is the nature and meaning of suffering. Without naming it as such—redemptive suffering—Derkx seeks to develop an understanding of human suffering that avoids a 'veil of soul-making' position whereby suffering has pedagogical merit, and he also doesn't want to deny the reality of suffering premised on moral evil.[2] Rather, he wants to understand human suffering as it relates to the negation of living well as being fostered through human activity and attitudes. His nontheistic humanism doesn't allow any other philosophical possibility. Humanism removes any divine sanction for misery; there is no cosmic mystery, and no cross as sign of redemptive suffering. Humanism, as defined by Derkx and so many others, pushes against theodicy and instead focuses on the challenges of anthropodicy. Based on this shift, he calls for a middle ground, wise tension between two poles, a "wise balance between accepting life as it is and striving for the possibility of a higher humanity. Humanity, as the way human beings are and as an ideal, never is just a solid fact to be taken for granted" (Derkx, 2013a, p. 57). The grammar for this binary is "progress and acceptance…between natality and mortality…" (Derkx, 2013a, p. 57), and all this is tested within the arena of longevity as a response to the "human condition" (Derkx, 2013a, p. 57). The manner in which Derkx positions the longevity conversation as a matter of science in relationship to ethics and morality cements together these binary positions and provides the under-girding logic and rationale.

Humanism and Longevity

I wonder about any effort to see pedagogical ramifications to suffering, anything that resembles learning to deal with suffering. Does that not easily bleed into learning to suffer? And does suffering function on the level of the individual (the mode of individualism he seems to support) over against collectives? In other words, what Derkx outlines requires a certain leisure of thought; but what of those whose context is defined by mechanisms of control that seek to break them down? In such a context, isn't it possible humanism becomes—like its theistic counterpoints—simply a means by which to come to terms with (rather than struggle against) human suffering? Put differently, it is possible this meaning frame called humanism functions like so many theistic theologies that serve as guides to life adjustment—guides to settling for the pain of human existence as

---

[2] For examples of this theodical position within the context of Christian thought, for example, see: John Hick, *Evil and the God of Love*, Reissue (New York: Palgrave Macmillan, 2010). Even liberation theologies fall victim to this mode of thinking: James H. Cone, *God of the Oppressed*, Revised Edition (Maryknoll, NY: Orbis Books, 1997); Gustavo Gutierrez, *On Job: God-Talk and the Suffering of the Innocent* (Maryknoll, NY: Orbis Books, 1987).

not only real but useful. Longevity, then, easily becomes a way of extending one's acquaintance with misery rather than destroying injustice. How does one avoid this situation?

It could be the case that this reading of Derkx on suffering and longevity isn't generous enough. After all, there is tied to life extension for Derkx moral and ethical considerations that have to do with who has access to technology as well as the conditions for those experiencing extended life. Clearly, much of the current interest in life extension involves at least an implicit fear of death and the process of dying (Derkx, 2009, p. 197). But underlying this concern with death, regardless of how longevity is configured, is a more general interest in 'more' productive time. Derkx thinks of this scenario in terms of two possibilities: Decelerated senescence whereby the markers of aging are slowed but not stopped, and arrested senescence whereby the processes of aging are controlled and treated which amounts to a modified mortality allowing people to live for what are now unimaginable periods of time (Derkx, 2009, pp. 199–200). But is the presumed sense of death undergirding these possibilities accurate? That is, should we think of death as a problem, as something to bracket off as distinct in a significant way from what we call 'life'?

While he does not advocate explicitly for such an understanding of death as distinct from life, his discussion of longevity fails to counter such claims. Cultural configurations of life seek to stem the tide of mortality by trying to control death, to quarantine it, so to speak, so as to give 'life' more vitality by handling death, by controlling it, ritualizing it, thinking it into a safe sphere of our historical circumstances. Something about the quest for longevity, for length of days, speaks to such a preoccupation with death as the dangerous 'foreigner' who threatens the integrity of our being. *More life, less death*—extended healthy existence and decreased biological destruction leading to demise.

It might be more useful to understand there is a significant connection between life and death. That is to say, we live into death. Such thinking poses thanatology as a challenge or even a corrective to technology: What does it mean to work (and use resources) to extend life, to manage or decrease attack on the biological integrity of the human, when death is not seen as foreign, as a problem to manage? There are social structures with economic and political consequence impinging on the length, quality, and meaning of life by which 'to live' doesn't mean the same thing across racial and gender lines. That is to say, for instance, socio-economic difficulties associated with racism and gender discrimination limit what certain individuals and certain groups can experience, the types of activities and arrangements of life (e.g., housing, medical care, and play) available to them. In such instance, to live and to survive are much more linked than they might be for more privileged classes. Yet, in many studies regarding extension of life, it appears the bodies under consideration are white and death is manageable as a problem set aside and apart.

There are concerns, situations of urgency, which extend well beyond the procedures needed to maintain long (and healthy) life. What of the cost involved? Without socio-economic and political transformation that decreases the reach of racial, gender, and other modalities of injustice, what is to be made of long life? As Derkx points out, while contested, many argue long life allows time to complete important 'projects'—but what does this mean for those for whom such projects take a back seat to the struggle for just the 'stuff' of basic survival? The extension of time to complete projects might just entail a degree of leisure and comfort unavailable to most (Derkx, 2009, pp. 204–6). To avoid skewing his argument as if it is devoid of existential considerations, it is important to note that Derkx does not fail to recognize the demand for justice as intimately connected to a meaningful life. "An important aspect of a meaningful life," he writes, "is that it can be justified morally, and one of the most important moral problems concerning the engineering of substantial life extension relates to justice" (Derkx, 2009, p. 207). And "all things considered it should be very difficult for human beings to enjoy a substantially extended and at the same time meaningful life without contributing anything to the fight against ethically unacceptable longevity inequalities in the world" (2009, p. 210). Still, his argument assumes moral benchmarks that are not clearly described and the demand for justice is not the final word in that the ability to extend life is not handicapped by the presence of injustice.

Derkx fails to acknowledge the full scope and impact of injustice. It doesn't only surface through shorter years of living or even quality of life measured in particular ways. Rich African Americans, for example, can still feel the pressures of race and gender discrimination—e.g., assumptions they aren't qualified, don't deserve the goods they purchase, and shouldn't be in the neighborhoods in which they live, or they are the target of police surveillance for 'driving while black.' This is to say the matrix of injustice is truncated and restricted in ways that artificially reduce the scope of its impact. So, "the existence of social injustice," he claims, "can never be a valid reason for morally objecting to any improvement in the fate of human beings who do not belong to the most underprivileged ones"

(Derkx, 2009, p. 208). Of course, it would be unreasonable to stifle technological advance because there is inequality in the world. Yet and still, can we afford to develop technology without a synergistic connection to justice? Derkx adjusts his discussion by qualifying justice as "perfect justice" (Derkx, 2013b, pp. 224–8). However, this is a false qualifier in that advancement with respect to justice should hold to a similar posture as that marking technological advancement: Not perfection, but steps that speak to improvement of a particular situation. Can humanism really embrace technological advance that doesn't demand an equal and simultaneous commitment to justice through the removal of barriers preventing access to and use of technology? Surely social constructs such as race have impacted access to medically advance procedures and medicines; and, race has also marked out populations for experimentation: Think of the Tuskegee experiment in the United States as one example of the manner in which issues of racial discrimination, for instance, have been tied to technological advancement for quite some time. How, then, can advancement take place without equal attention to justice? (e.g., Jones, 1993; Washington, 2008).

Derkx calls for "doing something" to address injustice (Derkx, 2013b, p. 209) so that all have access to technology that can enhance life. However, what does this mean, and what are the benchmarks of success? And shouldn't this quest for justice be tied in some substantial manner to technological advancement? Without a firm link between technological advance and the demands of justice, I fear, we lose our ability to distinguish quantity (of years) from quality (of years). Perhaps it is in this context that a positive tension between a meaningful and a happy life must be maintained as a marker of progress.

The Meaning of a Long Life

Some of my questions concerning justice are taken up in Derkx's work on a '*lingua democratica*' for genomics (Derkx, 2013b, pp. 209–42). By this, he means not a singular language that trumps linguistic context, but rather the development of a mechanism of communication and exchange that takes into consideration local communication strategies and meanings and uses this sensitivity to the local as a way of shaping appropriate contextually sound thinking and conversation regarding quality of life and life extension. It is a shared framework to be sure, but it is a language that recognizes the nature and import of local methods, and understands the significance of overlap and divergence of opinion, interests, and needs (Derkx, 2013b, pp. 210–11). For Derkx and his collaborators this democratic exchange acknowledges the need to think about genomics in ways that are mindful of the moral and ethical implications of such work.

There is 'bleed through' between discussions of aging and the sociopolitical and economic landscape of communities (Kunneman & Derkx, 2013, p. 7). Hence, this language is meant to provide a mechanism for robust and productive, public debate and exchange (Kunneman & Derkx, 2013, p. 11). In environments marked by shifting democratic grammars and practices, Derkx and his collaborators see opportunities for reviving the best dimensions of democracy. Still, what of injustice that marks legacies of democracy across the globe? What are the ways in which this *lingua democratica* accounts for and challenges status quo policies and practices of race, gender, class, sexuality, and so on that undoubtedly play out in the mechanisms of (de) aging? To what extent is it possible to speak of a *lingua democratica* within cultural contexts marked by localized grammars of disregard and abuse? Are such modes of linguistically arranged injustice part of the local linguistic landscapes that must be acknowledged (or maintained)? To what extent does this *lingua democratica* involve a process of opening public knowledge and debate on genomics, as opposed to the assumption such knowledge and debate is available but linguistically truncated? Who actually participates in these debates? What are the moral values highlighted within the framework and practice(s) of this *lingua democratica*?

Are All Things Equal?

There is an embedded optimism within this linguistic formulation, one that hints at the structuring of progress and mutuality downplaying or managing the realities of race, gender, class, sexuality, and other social constructs that shape experience of life and life's meaning. Derkx gets at such concerns through a question framing much of his research on aging: "Will it [longer human lifespan] benefit everybody equally?" (Derkx, 2013b, p. 209). As Derkx notes, genes account for a limited degree of the years of life experienced by an individual. Of greater importance are four factors he sums up this way: "nutrition, lifestyle (e.g., exercise, excessive food, social isolation), environment (e.g., education, housing and income) and chance" (Derkx, 2013b, pp. 210–11). And some of these factors are not disassociated from social constructions such as race and gender. Longevity, then, is influenced in a significant manner by issues neatly captured through attention to issues of justice and injustice as they relate to the impact of race and gender on the first three of four factors. By extension, what is meant by morbidity and how it might be 'massaged' and whether increased number of years—and how many years—is the primary concern, has limited value within a context in which various modalities of injustice provide cultural circumstances creating suspicion and limited contact with technological innovations.

Technological advances are already and always 'colored' and gendered, reflecting the cultural worlds in which they take place. The question, then, has to involve how to address the inadequacies of those social constructions marking our cultural worlds so as to allow for the most useful and far-reaching technologies possible. I would suggest—no argue—there is no possibility of equitable access to technology without explicit and sustained attention to modes of inequality and injustice. And, a willingness to so engage is dependent on numerous factors that must be made explicit and central:

1. A desire to maintain synergy between technology and justice. One way to think about firming up this link is to more aggressively recruit women and so-called racial minorities into STEAM disciplines within universities and colleges (Science, Technology, Engineering, the Arts, and Mathematics). In addition, this would also entail making certain resources are in place that allow students from economically challenged schools to gain the skills and backgrounds necessary to do advanced work in STEAM disciplines on the collegiate level. As part of this process, universities and colleges would need to provide programs that aim to encourage participation in STEAM fields and that help students, who have talent, address any deficiencies.
2. The will to see investment in justice work as grounding for technological advance. This might involve the development of community-based programs that finance, encourage, and reward grounded technology—that is technology that addresses explicitly the conditions of life within disadvantaged communities.
3. Maintaining of a moral and ethical litmus test for assessing technological advance—including solid concern with the integrity of embodied bodies brought into play as part of the scientific infrastructure. Included here would be explicit focus on moral and ethical outcomes and processes built into grant applications, STEAM courses, and so on.

4. A grammar of quality of life sensitive to the nature and impact of social construction(s) of identity. Ways to speak about technology and social life need to make sense to those most deeply impacted by technological inequality, and it needs to be mindful of the sociocultural signifiers that have been used to determine and shape the assumed values and 'rights' of disadvantaged communities.
5. Disciplined and authorized mechanisms of oversight that use as a criterion issues and their consequences for social justice. The direction and aim of technological advances must be measured against their impact on issues of social justice and equality. The manner in which 'success' is noted and measured should reflect a concern with issues of social justice and equality. (Derkx, 2013b, pp. 224–35)

Mindful of the above, there is a problem requiring attention. Derkx phrases the dilemma this way: "Decisions to try to extend human life substantially for the time being will very much be political or corporate decisions, for instance about priorities in biomedical research. Thus, taking autonomy seriously comes down to taking liberal democracy and citizenship seriously" (Derkx, 2013b, p. 219). Short of such a structured approach, one is assuming an interest in the moral and ethical dimensions of technology having the wherewithal to resist the temptations of economic and political pay-off. This is an unwise and unsafe assumption, indeed! The historical record of too many countries points to tragic episodes of economic, ideological, and political motivations trumping the well-being of humans and other animals.

Furthermore, how are issues of social injustice addressed when certain populations—e.g., African Americans—have been ontologized and epistemologically arranged as disease to be quarantined? That is to say, racism within the United States (although not restricted to this particular nation/state) seeks to bracket Black bodies so as to render them docile, to control and shift them in ways that speak to White supremacy logic.[3] This has involved treating African Americans on so many occasions as a threat to the health and well-being of the dominant population.

---

[3] The postmodernist undertones of my thinking here are evident. And, while Derkx, wants to caution against too strong a turn in that direction, I believe the perspective on the nature of both discursive and material bodies offered through postmodern sensibilities are helpful here.

Segregation is only one of the ways in which this pathologizing of African Americans plays out and, I would assert, similar processes of geographic quarantine take place elsewhere in the world and these locations take on a variety of names—ghetto being just one of the more readily understood. The parsing out of populations through a grammar of virus surely has some bearing on the nature of life meaning as a humanist concern. But, in addition to this, the ways in which technology for life extension (and improvement in a general sense) is measured, tested, and meted out takes place under the shadow of practices of dehumanization and a questionable ethos of pathology.

Final Thoughts

How does one talk about the moral and ethical connotations of morbidity and longevity within dehumanizing contexts of life encountered by so many? Doing so, at the very least, requires pushing beyond the abstract, generic 'humans' and their issues of senescence to particular embodied humans who are marked by signifiers of race, gender, class, and so on. Addressing cancer as a way of extending morbidity without attention, for instance, to environmental racism that exposes particular populations to significant pollutants limits the reach of technological advances.

The United States, for instance, isn't simply 'greying' it is also 'browning,' and what does this entail for discussion of life, life meaning, and life extension? Or, how do we discuss the value of nutrition for life extension in the context of food deserts? Is it enough to label social injustice as moral issue within the discourse on life extension? Does this give it the intimate connection to technological advance necessary to promote justice? I would suggest, no.

Address root causes, rather than symptoms. While surely a moral and ethical concern, issues of social justice inform the development and distribution of technology only to the extent justice is marked as fundamentally connected to the mission and purpose of technological advance. More than "social responsibility and political will" (Derkx, 2013b, p. 226) are required to prioritize social justice as fundamental to the development and distribution of technologies of life. Technological advance must have a binary framing—advancing quality and length of life and reducing the 'stuff' that hampers—based on discrimination and injustice—human flourishing. In fairness to Derkx, he does see this as an important point: This creative tension is more than plausible. The challenge involves ways to realize this tension, as well as methods by means of which to ensure this creative synergy is present as a foundational mechanism for both conceiving and practicing longevity technology.

Derkx asks if life-extension is desirable, and the answer depends on to whom the question is posed. What is a "just and humane society"? (Derkx, 2013b, p. 234). Likewise, the answer to this question is dependent upon the person to whom it is posed. Contextual questions demand context-sensitive answers. The perception of technology also depends on the socio-cultural vantage point from which it is posed. There is much that can 'color' perception of technology, pun intended. In a similar vein, to the extent gender is performed, with the markers of gender transferable, what life means and what technology hampers depends on the manner in which gender dynamics are rehearsed. What, then, is normative?

Meaning—life meaning—is contextual, layered, and dependent on the manner in which bodies occupy time and space. And, what is thought about extending life as a matter of meaning enhancement is already and always tied to the cultural worlds from within which, as my grandmother would say, quoting scripture, we "live, move, and have our being." To think otherwise might just entail a **li**(f)**e** we can't afford to tell, if well-being is actually of primary concern.

Bibliography

Derkx, P. (2009) 'Substantial life extension and meanings of life', in Willem B. Drees (Ed.), *Technology, trust, and religion: Roles of religions in controversies on ecology and the modification of life* (pp. 197–220). Leiden University Press.

Derkx, P. (2013a). Humanism as a meaning frame. In A. B. Pinn (Ed.), *What is humanism and why does it matter?* (pp. 42–57). Acumen.

Derkx, P. (2013b). Worldviews, genomics and enhanced human lifespan. In P. Derkx & H. Kunneman (Eds.), *Genomics and democracy: Towards a 'lingua democratica' for the public debate on genomics* (pp. 209–242). Rodopi.

Jones, J. H. (1993). *Bad blood: The Tuskegee syphilis experiment.* The Free Press.

Kunneman, H., & Derkx, P. (2013). Introduction. In P. Derkx & H. Kunneman (Eds.), *Genomics and democracy: Towards a 'lingua Democratica' for the public debate on genomics* (pp. 7–33). Rodopi.

Lamont, C. (1997). *The philosophy of humanism.* The Humanist Press.

Washington, H. A. (2008). *Medical apartheid: The dark history of medical experimentation on Black Americans from colonial times to the present.* Anchor.

Bibliography

Achenbaum, W. A. (1995). *Crossing frontiers: Gerontology emerges as a science.* Cambridge University Press.

Ahmadi Lewin, F. (2001). Gerotranscendence and different cultural settings. *Ageing and Society, 21,* 395–415.

Alma, H., & Smaling, A. (Eds.). (2010). *Waarvoor je leeft: studies naar humanistische bronnen van zin.* SWP, Humanistic University Press.

Antonovsky, A. (1987). *Unraveling the mystery of health: How people manage stress and stay well.* Jossey-Bass.

Antonucci, T. C., & Webster, N. J. (2019). Involvement with life and social networks: A pathway for successful aging. In R. Fernandez-Ballesteros, A. Benetos, & J. Robine (Eds.), *The Cambridge handbook of successful aging* (pp. 475–491). Cambridge University Press.

Apostel, L. (1998). Een ander geloven. Een nieuw transcenderen. Over niet-theïstische spiritualiteit [1994]. In *Atheïstische spiritualiteit* (pp. 23–37). VUBPRESS.

Arutyunova, K. R., Alexandrov, Y. I., & Hauser, M. D. (2016). Sociocultural influences on moral judgments: East-west, male-female, and young-old. *Frontiers in Psychology, 7*(September, Article 1334), 1–15.

Atchley, R. C. (2009). *Spirituality and aging.* The Johns Hopkins University Press.

Atchley, R. C. (2011). How spiritual experience and development interact with aging. *The Journal of Transpersonal Psychology, 43*(2), 156–165.

Atchley, R. C. (2016). Spirituality and ageing: Yesterday, today and tomorrow. In M. Johnson & J. Walker (Eds.), *Spiritual dimensions of ageing* (pp. 13–31). Cambridge University Press.

Baars, J. (2010). Philosophy of aging, time, and finitude. In T. R. Cole, R. E. Ray, & R. Kastenbaum (Eds.), *A guide to humanistic studies in aging: What does it mean to grow old?* (pp. 105–120). The Johns Hopkins University Press.

Bakan, D. (1966). *The duality of human existence: Isolation and communion in Western man.* Beacon Press.

Battista, J., & Almond, R. (1973). The development of meaning in life. *Psychiatry, 36,* 409–427.

Bauer, J. J., Schwab, J. R., & McAdams, D. P. (2011). Self-actualizing: Where ego development finally feels good? *The Humanistic Psychologist, 39,* 121–136.

Baumeister, R. F. (1991). *Meanings of life.* Guilford Press.

Baumeister, R. F., & Vohs, K. D. (2018). Revisiting our reappraisal of the (surprisingly few) benefits of high self-esteem. *Perspectives on Psychological Science, 13*(2), 137–140.

Baumeister, R. F., Vohs, K. D., Aaker, J. L., & Garbinsky, E. N. (2013). Some key differences between a happy life and a meaningful life. *The Journal of Positive Psychology, 8*(6), 505–516.

Bercovitz, K. E., Ngnoumen, C., & Langer, E. J. (2019). Personal control and successful aging. In R. Fernandez-Ballesteros, A. Benetos, & J. Robine (Eds.), *The Cambridge handbook of successful aging* (pp. 384–400). Cambridge University Press.

Berlin, I. (1991). The pursuit of the ideal. In *The crooked timber of humanity: Chapters in the history of ideas* (pp. 1–19). HarperCollins, Fontana Press.

Braam, A. W., Galenkamp, H., Derkx, P., Aartsen, M. J., & Deeg, D. J. H. (2016). Ten-year course of cosmic transcendence in older adults in The Netherlands. *The International Journal of Aging and Human Development, 84*(1), 44–65. https://doi.org/10.1177/0091415016668354

Carstensen, L. L. (1995). Evidence for a life-span theory of socioemotional selectivity. *Current Directions in Psychological Science, 4*(5), 151–156.

Carstensen, L. L., Isaacowitz, D. M., & Charles, S. T. (1999). Taking time seriously: A theory of socioemotional selectivity. *American Psychologist, 54*(3), 165–181.

Colby, A., Bundick, M., Remington, K., & Morton, E. (2020). Moral flourishing in later life through purpose beyond the self. In L. A. Jensen (Ed.), *The Oxford handbook of moral development: An interdisciplinary perspective* (pp. 1–24). Oxford University Press.

Cole, T. R. (1992). *The journey of life: A cultural history of aging in America.* Cambridge University Press.

Coleman, P.G. and colleagues, University of Southampton (Ed.). (2011). *Belief and ageing: Spiritual pathways in later life.* The Policy Press.

Coleman, P. G., Ivani-Chalian, C., & Robinson, M. (2015). *Self and meaning in the lives of older people*. Cambridge University Press.
Côté, S., Piff, P. K., & Willer, R. (2013). For whom do the ends justify the means? Social class and utilitarian moral judgment. *Journal of Personality and Social Psychology, 104*(3), 490–503.
Crescioni, A. W., & Baumeister, R. F. (2013). The four needs for meaning, the value gap, and how (and whether) society can fill the void. In J. A. Hicks & C. Routledge (Eds.), *The experience of meaning in life: Classical perspectives, emerging themes, and controversies* (pp. 3–15). Springer.
Crumbaugh, J. C., & Maholick, L. T. (1967). An experimental study in existentialism: The psychometric approach to Frankl's concept of noögenic neurosis. In V. E. Frankl (Ed.), *Psychotherapy and existentialism: Selected papers on logotherapy* (pp. 183–197). Simon and Schuster.
Dannefer, D. (1999). Neoteny, naturalization, and other constituents of human development. In C. D. Ryff & V. W. Marshall (Eds.), *The self and society in aging processes* (pp. 67–93). Springer.
de St. Aubin, E. (2013). Generativity and the meaning of life. In J. A. Hicks & C. Routledge (Eds.), *The experience of meaning in life: Classical perspectives, emerging themes, and controversies* (pp. 241–255). Springer.
de St. Aubin, E., & Bach, M. (2014). Explorations in generativity and culture. In L. A. Jensen (Ed.), *The Oxford handbook of human development and culture: An interdisciplinary perspective* (pp. 1–21). Oxford University Press.
Derkx, P. (2009) 'Substantial life extension and meanings of life', in Willem B. Drees (Ed.), Technology, trust, and religion: Roles of religions in controversies on ecology and the modification of life (pp. 197–220). Leiden University Press.
Derkx, P. (2011). *Humanisme, zinvol leven en nooit meer 'ouder worden': een levensbeschouwelijke visie op ingrijpende biomedisch-technologische levensverlenging*. ASP, VUBPRESS.
Derkx, P. (2013a). Humanism as a meaning frame. In A. B. Pinn (Ed.), *What is humanism and why does it matter?* (pp. 42–57). Acumen.
Derkx, P. (2013b). Worldviews, genomics and enhanced human lifespan. In P. Derkx & H. Kunneman (Eds.), *Genomics and democracy: Towards a 'lingua democratica' for the public debate on genomics* (pp. 209–242). Rodopi.
Derkx, P. (2015). The future of humanism. In A. Copson & A. C. Grayling (Eds.), *The Wiley Blackwell handbook of humanism* (pp. 426–439). Wiley Blackwell.
Derkx, P. (2016). A humanist evaluation of substantial life extension through biomedical research and technology. In A. B. Pinn (Ed.), *Humanism and technology, studies in humanism and atheism* (pp. 99–122). Palgrave Macmillan.
Derkx, P. (2018). Het blijft mensenwerk: een humanistische visie op spirituele dimensies van goed ouder worden. *Waardenwerk, 72*(mei), 59–76.

Derkx, P., Bos, P., Laceulle, H., & Machielse, A. (2020). Meaning in life and the experience of older people. *International Journal of Ageing and Later Life*, *14*(1), 37–66.
Derkx, P., & Laceulle, H. (2021). Humanism and aging. In A. B. Pinn (Ed.), *The Oxford handbook of humanism* (pp. 665–694). Oxford University Press.
de Vries, B. (2010). The value and meaning of friendship in later life. In T. R. Cole, R. E. Ray, & R. Kastenbaum (Eds.), *A guide to humanistic studies in aging: What does it mean to grow old?* (pp. 141–162). The Johns Hopkins University Press.
Diener, E., & Diener, C. (1996). Most people are happy. *Psychological Science*, *7*(3), 181–185.
Diener, E., Lucas, R. E., & Scollon, C. N. (2006). Beyond the hedonic treadmill: Revising the adaptation theory of well-being. *American Psychologist*, *61*(4), 305–314.
Diener, E., Scollon, C. N., & Lucas, R. E. (2009). The evolving concept of subjective well-being: The multifaceted nature of happiness [2004]. In E. Diener (Ed.), *Assessing well-being: The collected works of Ed Diener* (pp. 67–100). Springer.
Dykstra, P. A. (2009). Older adult loneliness: Myths and realities. *European Journal of Ageing*, *6*(2), 91–100.
Dykstra, P. A., van Tilburg, T. G., & de Jong Gierveld, J. (2005). Changes in older adult loneliness: Results from a seven-year longitudinal study. *Research on Aging*, *27*(6), 725–747.
Edmondson, R. (2015). *Ageing, insight and wisdom: Meaning and practice across the lifecourse*. The Policy Press.
Erikson, E. H. (1985). *The life cycle completed: A review*. Originally published 1982. W. W. Norton.
Erikson, E. H. (1986). *Childhood and society* (1st ed. 1950; 2nd ed. 1963); Afterthoughts 1985; Reissued 1993. W. W. Norton.
Erikson, E. H., & Erikson, J. M. (1978). Introduction: Reflections on aging. In S. F. Spicker, K. M. Woodward, & D. D. Van Tassel (Eds.), *Aging and the elderly: Humanistic perspectives in gerontology* (pp. 1–8). Humanities Press.
Erikson, E. H., & Erikson, J. M. (1998). *The life cycle completed: Extended version with new chapters on the ninth stage of development by Joan M. Erikson*. W. W. Norton.
Eriksson, M. (2017). The sense of coherence in the salutogenic model of health. In M. B. Mittelmark, S. Sagy, M. Eriksson, G. F. Bauer, J. M. Pelikan, B. Lindstrom, & G. A. Espnes (Eds.), *The handbook of salutogenesis* (pp. 91–96). Springer.
Fokkema, T., de Jong Gierveld, J., & Dykstra, P. A. (2012). Cross-national differences in older adult loneliness. *The Journal of Psychology*, *146*(1–2), 201–228.
Fowler, J. (2015). Spirituality. In A. Copson & A. C. Grayling (Eds.), *The Wiley Blackwell handbook of humanism* (pp. 347–373). Wiley Blackwell.

Frankl, V. E. (2006). *Man's search for meaning* [First published in German in 1946]. Beacon Press.
Freeman, M. (2010). Afterword. 'Even amidst': Rethinking narrative coherence. In M. Hyvarinen, L. Hyden, M. Saarenheimo, & M. Tamboukou (Eds.), *Beyond narrative coherence* (pp. 167–186). John Benjamins.
Freund, A. M., & Baltes, P. B. (1998). Selection, optimization, and compensation as strategies of life management: Correlations with subjective indicators of successful aging. *Psychology and Aging, 13*(4), 531–543.
Fung, H. H., & Carstensen, L. L. (2006). Goals change when life's fragility is primed: Lessons learned from older adults, the September 11 attacks and SARS. *Social Cognition, 24*(3), 248–278.
Gecas, V., & Seff, M. A. (1990). Social class and self-esteem: Psychological centrality, compensation, and the relative effects of work and home. *Social Psychology Quarterly, 53*(2; June; Special Issue: Social Structure and the Individual), 165–173.
Ginzburg, C. (1992). *The cheese and the worms: The cosmos of a sixteenth-century miller*. Johns Hopkins University Press.
Glenn, N. D. (2003). Distinguishing age, period, and cohort effects. In J. T. Mortimer & M. J. Shanahan (Eds.), *Handbook of the life course* (pp. 465–476). Kluwer Academic / Plenum Publishers.
Gullette, M. M. (2010). Ageism and social change: The new regimes of decline. In T. R. Cole, R. E. Ray, & R. Kastenbaum (Eds.), *A guide to humanistic studies in aging: What does it mean to grow old?* (pp. 319–340). The Johns Hopkins University Press.
Heine, S. J., Lehman, D. R., Markus, H. R., & Kitayama, S. (1999). Is there a universal need for positive self-regard? *Psychological Review, 106*(4), 766–794.
Heintzelman, S. J., Trent, J., & King, L. A. (2013). Encounters with objective coherence and the experience of meaning in life. *Psychological Science, 24*, 991–998.
Hicks, J. A., & Routledge, C. (Eds.). (2013). *The experience of meaning in life: Classical perspectives, emerging themes, and controversies*. Springer.
Hindriks, F. (2015). How does reasoning (fail to) contribute to moral judgment? Dumbfounding and disengagement. *Ethical Theory and Moral Practice, 18*, 237–250.
Hofer, J., Busch, H., Au, A., Solcova, I. P., Tavel, P., & Wong, T. T. (2014). For the benefit of others: Generativity and meaning in life in the elderly in four cultures. *Psychology and Aging, 29*(4), 764–775.
Holt-Lunstad, J. (2018). Relationships and physical health. In A. L. Vangelisti & D. Perlman (Eds.), *The Cambridge handbook of personal relationships* (2nd ed., pp. 449–463). Cambridge University Press.
Inglis, T. (2014). *Meanings of life in contemporary Ireland*. Palgrave Macmillan.

Irving, J., Davis, S., & Collier, A. (2017). Aging with purpose: Systematic search and review of literature pertaining to older adults and purpose. *The International Journal of Aging and Human Development, 85*(4), 403–437.
Janoff-Bulman, R., & Yopyk, D. J. (2004). Random outcomes and valued commitments: Existential dilemmas and the paradox of meaning. In J. Greenberg, S. L. Koole, & T. Pyszczynski (Eds.), *Handbook of experimental existential psychology* (pp. 125–141). The Guilford Press.
Johnson, M. (2016). Spirituality, biographical review and biographical pain at the end of life in old age. In M. Johnson & J. Walker (Eds.), *Spiritual dimensions of ageing* (pp. 198–214). Cambridge University Press.
Johnson, M., & Walker, J. (Eds.). (2016). *Spiritual dimensions of ageing.* Cambridge University Press.
Jones, J. H. (1993). *Bad blood: The Tuskegee syphilis experiment.* The Free Press.
Keyes, C. L. M. (1998). Social well-being. *Social Psychology Quarterly, 61*(2), 121–140.
Keyes, C. L. M., & Shapiro, A. D. (2004). Social well-being in the United States: A descriptive epidemiology. In O. G. Brim, C. D. Ryff, & R. C. Kessler (Eds.), *How healthy are we? A national study of well-being at midlife* (pp. 350–372). The University of Chicago Press.
Keyes, C. L. M., Shmotkin, D., & Ryff, C. D. (2002). Optimizing well-being: The empirical encounter of two traditions. *Journal of Personality and Social Psychology, 82*(6), 1007–1022.
King, L. A., & Hicks, J. A. (2007). Whatever happened to 'what might have been'? Regrets, happiness, and maturity. *American Psychologist, 62*(7), 625–636.
King, L. A., & Hicks, J. A. (2009). Detecting and constructing meaning in life events. *The Journal of Positive Psychology, 5*(5), 317–330.
King, L. A., Heintzelman, S. J., & Ward, S. J. (2016). Beyond the search for meaning: A contemporary science of the experience of meaning in life. *Current Directions in Psychological Science, 25*(4), 211–216.
Klemke, E. D., & Cahn, S. M. (Eds.). (2008). *The meaning of life: A reader* (3rd ed.). Oxford University Press.
Kohn, M. L. (1989). Social structure and personality: A quintessentially sociological approach to social psychology. *Social Forces, 68*(1), 26–33.
Kotre, J. (1984). *Outliving the self: Generativity and the interpretation of lives.* The Johns Hopkins University Press.
Kruse, A., & Schmitt, E. (2019). Spirituality and transcendence. In R. Fernandez-Ballesteros, A. Benetos, & J. Robine (Eds.), *The Cambridge handbook of successful aging* (pp. 426–454). Cambridge University Press.
Laceulle, H. (2013). Self-realisation and ageing: A spiritual perspective. In J. Baars, J. Dohmen, A. Grenier, & C. Phillipson (Eds.), *Ageing, meaning and social structure: Connecting critical and humanistic gerontology* (pp. 97–118). The Policy Press.

Laceulle, H. (2017). Virtuous aging and existential vulnerability. *Journal of Aging Studies, 43*(December), 1–8.
Laceulle, H. (2018). *Aging and self-realization: Cultural narratives about later life*. transcript.
Laceulle, H., & Baars, J. (2014). Self-realization and cultural narratives about later life. *Journal of Aging Studies, 31*(December), 34–44.
Lamont, C. (1997). *The philosophy of humanism*. The Humanist Press.
Machielse, A., & Hortulanus, R. (2013). Social ability or social frailty? The balance between autonomy and connectedness in the lives of older people. In J. Baars, J. Dohmen, A. Grenier, & C. Phillipson (Eds.), *Ageing, meaning and social structure: Connecting critical and humanistic gerontology* (pp. 119–138). The Policy Press.
MacKinlay, E. (2016). Ageing and spirituality across faiths and cultures. In M. Johnson & J. Walker (Eds.), *Spiritual dimensions of ageing* (pp. 32–50). Cambridge University Press.
Martela, F. (2020). *A wonderful life: Insights on finding a meaningful existence*. Harper Collins.
Martela, F., & Steger, M. F. (2016). The three meanings of meaning in life: Distinguishing coherence, purpose, and significance. *The Journal of Positive Psychology, 11*(5), 531–545.
Mathews, G. (1996). *What makes life worth living? How Japanese and Americans make sense of their worlds*. University of California Press.
May, T. (2015). *A significant life: Human meaning in a silent universe*. The University of Chicago Press.
McAdams, D. P. (1997). *The stories we live by: Personal myths and the making of the self*. The Guilford Press.
McNair, S., Okan, Y., Hadjichristidis, C., & Bruine de Bruin, W. (2019). Age differences in moral judgment: Older adults are more deontological than younger adults. *Journal of Behavioral Decision Making, 32*, 47–60.
Melton, A. M. A., & Schulenberg, S. E. (2007). On the relationship between meaning in life and boredom proneness: Examining a logotherapy postulate. *Psychological Reports, 101*, 1016–1022.
Minois, G. (1989). *History of old age: From antiquity to the renaissance*. The University of Chicago Press.
Miyamoto, Y., Yoo, J., Levine, C. S., Park, J., Boylan, J. M., Sims, T., Markus, H. R., Kitayama, S., Kawakami, N., Karasawa, M., Coe, C. L., Love, G. D., & Ryff, C. D. (2018). Culture and social hierarchy: Self- and other-oriented correlates of socioeconomic status across cultures. *Journal of Personality and Social Psychology, 115*(3), 427–445.
Mooren, J. H. (1998). Zingeving en cognitieve regulatie: een conceptueel model ten behoeve van onderzoek naar zingeving en levensbeschouwing. In J. Janssen, R. van Uden, & H. van der Ven (Eds.), *Schering en inslag: opstellen over religie*

in de hedendaagse cultuur (pp. 193–206). Katholiek Studiecentrum voor Geestelijke Volksgezondheid (KSGV).
Morgan, J., & Farsides, T. (2009). Measuring meaning in life. *Journal of Happiness Studies, 10*(3), 197–214.
Mroczek, D. K., & Kolarz, C. M. (1998). The effect of age on positive and negative affect: A developmental perspective on happiness. *Journal of Personality and Social Psychology, 75*(5), 1333–1349.
Orth, U., Erol, R. Y., & Luciano, E. C. (2018). Development of self-esteem from age 4 to 94 years: A meta-analysis of longitudinal studies. *Psychological Bulletin, 144*(10), 1045–1080.
Park, H. W. (2016). *Old age, new science: Gerontologists and their biosocial visions, 1900–1960*. University of Pittsburgh Press.
Piff, P. K. (2014). Wealth and the inflated self: Class, entitlement, and narcissism. *Personality and Social Psychology Bulletin, 40*(1), 34–43.
Pinquart, M. (2002). Creating and maintaining purpose in life in old age: A meta-analysis. *Ageing International, 27*(2), 90–114.
Popper, K. R. (1989). On the status of science and of metaphysics [1958]. In *Conjectures and refutations: The growth of scientific knowledge* (5th revised ed.; pp. 184–200). Routledge.
Pratt, M. W., Matsuba, M. K., Lawford, H. L., & Villar, F. (2020). The life span development of generativity. In L. A. Jensen (Ed.), *The Oxford handbook of moral development: An interdisciplinary perspective* (pp. 1–24). Oxford University Press.
Riediger, M., Li, S., & Lindenberger, U. (2006). Selection, optimization, and compensation as developmental mechanisms of adaptive resource allocation: Review and preview. In J. E. Birren, K. W. Schaie, R. P. Abeles, M. Gatz, & T. A. Salthouse (Eds.), *Handbook of the psychology of aging* (6th ed., pp. 289–313). Elsevier, Academic Press.
Riley, M. W., Kahn, R. L., & Foner, A. (Eds.). (1994). *Age and structural lag: Society's failure to provide meaningful opportunities in work, family, and leisure*. John Wiley & Sons.
Robinson, S. A., & Lachman, M. E. (2017). Perceived control and aging: A mini-review and directions for future research. *Gerontology, 63*, 435–442.
Ronkes Agerbeek, I. (2016). *Je hebt jezelf gevonden, als je jezelf ook durft te verliezen: Interdisciplinair theoretisch onderzoek naar de waarde van het nastreven van een moreel zelfbeeld als bron van eigenwaarde en zin*. University of Humanistic Studies.
Ryan, R. M., & Deci, E. L. (2001). On happiness and human potentials: A review of research on hedonic and eudaimonic well-being. *Annual Review of Psychology, 52*, 141–166.

Ryff, C. D. (1989). Happiness is everything, or is it? Explorations on the meaning of psychological well-being. *Journal of Personality and Social Psychology, 57*(6), 1069–1081.

Ryff, C. D. (2014). Psychological well-being revisited: Advances in the science and practice of eudaimonia. *Psychotherapy and Psychosomatics, 83*(1), 10–28.

Ryff, C. D. (2017). Eudaimonic well-being, inequality, and health: Recent findings and future directions. *International Review of Economics, 64*(2), 159–178.

Ryff, C. D., Keyes, C. L. M., & Hughes, D. L. (2004). Psychological well-being in MIDUS: Profiles of ethnic/racial diversity and life-course uniformity. In O. G. Brim, C. D. Ryff, & R. C. Kessler (Eds.), *How healthy are we? A national study of well-being at midlife* (pp. 398–422). The University of Chicago Press.

Ryff, C. D., Love, G. D., Miyamoto, Y., Markus, H. R., Curhan, K. B., Kitayama, S., Park, J., Kawakami, N., Kan, C., & Karasawa, M. (2014). Culture and the promotion of well-being in east and west: Understanding varieties of attunement to the surrounding context. In G. A. Fava & C. Ruini (Eds.), *Increasing psychological well-being in clinical and educational settings: Interventions and cultural contexts* (pp. 1–19). Springer.

Schoklitsch, A., & Baumann, U. (2012). Generativity and aging: A promising future research topic? *Journal of Aging Studies, 26*, 262–272.

Schooler, C., Mulatu, M. S., & Oates, G. (2004). Occupational self-direction, intellectual functioning, and self-directed orientation in older workers: Findings and implications for individuals and societies. *American Journal of Sociology, 110*(1), 161–197.

Schwartz, S. H., Cieciuch, J., Vecchione, M., Davidov, E., Fischer, R., Beierlein, C., Ramos, A., Verkasalo, M., Lonnqvist, J., Demirutku, K., Dirilen-Gumus, O., & Konty, M. (2012). Refining the theory of basic individual values. *Journal of Personality and Social Psychology, 103*(4), 663–688.

Shmotkin, D. (2011). The pursuit of happiness: Alternative conceptions of subjective well-being. In L. W. Poon & J. Cohen-Mansfield (Eds.), *Understanding well-being in the oldest old* (pp. 27–45). Cambridge University Press.

Shmotkin, D., & Shrira, A. (2012). On the distinction between subjective well-being and meaning in life: Regulatory versus reconstructive functions in the face of a hostile world. In P. T. P. Wong (Ed.), *The human quest for meaning: Theories, research, and applications* (2nd ed., pp. 143–163). Taylor & Francis, Routledge.

Shmotkin, D., & Shrira, A. (2013). Subjective well-being and meaning in life in a hostile world: Proposing a configurative perspective. In J. A. Hicks & C. Routledge (Eds.), *The experience of meaning in life: Classical perspectives, emerging themes, and controversies* (pp. 77–86). Springer.

Shmotkin, D., Shrira, A., Eyal, N., Blumstein, T., & Shorek, A. (2013). The prediction of subjective wellness among the old-old: Implications for the "fourth-age" conception. *Journals of Gerontology, Series B: Psychological Sciences and Social Sciences, 69*(5), 719–729.

Shrira, A., Palgi, Y., Ben-Ezra, M., & Shmotkin, D. (2011). How subjective well-being and meaning in life interact in the hostile world. *The Journal of Positive Psychology, 6*(4), 273–285.

Smaling, A., & Alma, H. (2010). Zingeving en levensbeschouwing: een conceptuele en thematische verkenning. In H. Alma & A. Smaling (Eds.), *Waarvoor je leeft: studies naar humanistische bronnen van zin* (pp. 17–39). SWP, Humanistic University Press.

Specht, J., Egloff, B., & Schmukle, S. C. (2013). Everything under control? The effects of age, gender, and education on trajectories of perceived control in a nationally representative German sample. *Developmental Psychology, 49*(2), 353–364.

Steger, M. F. (2018). Meaning in life: A unified model. In C. R. Snyder, S. J. Lopez, L. M. Edwards, & S. C. Marques (Eds.), *The Oxford handbook of positive psychology* (3rd ed., 15 pp). Oxford University Press.

Sternberg, R. J. (1986). A triangular theory of love. *Psychological Review, 93*(2), 119–135.

Stillman, T. F., & Lambert, N. M. (2013). The bidirectional relationship of meaning and belonging. In J. A. Hicks & C. Routledge (Eds.), *The experience of meaning in life: Classical perspectives, emerging themes, and controversies* (pp. 305–315). Springer.

Streeter, J. L., Raposo, S., & Liao, H. (2016). The importance of social relationships for longevity. In *Social Engagement (Sightlines Project Special Report)*. Stanford Center on Longevity, pp. 1–29.

Thane, P. (2000). *Old age in English history: Past experiences, present issues*. Oxford University Press.

Thompson, S. C. (2017). The role of personal control in adaptive functioning. In C. R. Snyder, S. J. Lopez, L. M. Edwards, & S. C. Marques (Eds.), *The Oxford handbook of positive psychology* (3rd ed., 22 pp). Oxford University Press.

Tiberius, V. (2015). *Moral psychology: A contemporary introduction*. Routledge.

Tornstam, L. (1997a). Gerotranscendence: The contemplative dimension of aging. *Journal of Aging Studies, 11*(2), 143–154.

Tornstam, L. (1997b). Life crises and gerotranscendence. *Journal of Aging and Identity, 2*, 117–131.

Tornstam, L. (2005). *Gerotranscendence: A developmental theory of positive aging*. Springer.

Tsai, J. L., Sims, T., Qu, Y., Thomas, E., Jiang, D., & Fung, H. H. (2018). Valuing excitement makes people look forward to old age less and dread it more. *Psychology and Aging, 33*(7), 975–992.

van Luijk, H. (1979). Karl-Otto Apel en de grondslagen van de ethiek. *Tijdschrift voor Filosofie, 41*(1), 35–67.

van Praag, J. P. (1982). *Foundations of humanism*. Prometheus Books.
van de Goor, J., Sools, A. M., & Westerhof, G. J. (2019). Unraveling the wonder of the ordinary: A narrative analysis of meaning construction in memories of familiar routines. *Journal of Constructivist Psychology, 32*(3), 292–308.
van de Goor, J., Sools, A. M., Westerhof, G. J., & Bohlmeijer, E. T. (2020). Wonderful life: Exploring wonder in meaningful moments. *Journal of Humanistic Psychology, 60*(2), 147–167.
van der Vaart, W., Arisse, E., Weijers, C., & van Elteren, A. (2015). *Een exploratie van inhoud en methoden voor een kwaliteitstandaard 'Omgaan met levensvragen in de langdurende zorg voor ouderen'. De tweede onderzoeksfase*. Universiteit voor Humanistiek.
Vaupel, J. W., & Loichinger, E. (2006). Redistributing work in aging Europe. *Science, 312*(30), 1911–1913.
von Faber, M., Bootsma-van der Wiel, A., van Exel, E., Gusseklo, J., Lagaay, A. M., van Dongen, E., Knook, D. L., van der Geest, S., & Westendorp, R. G. J. (2001). Successful aging in the oldest old: Who can be characterized as successfully aged? *Archives of Internal Medicine, 161*(10/24), 2694–2700.
Walker, L. J., & Frimer, J. A. (2015). Developmental trajectories of agency and communion in moral motivation. *Merrill-Palmer Quarterly, 61*(3), 412–439.
Washington, H. A. (2008). *Medical apartheid: The dark history of medical experimentation on Black Americans from colonial times to the present*. Anchor.
Wolf, S. (2010). *Meaning in life and why it matters* (Introduction by S. Macedo; with commentary by J. Koethe, R. M. Adams, N. Arpaly, & J. Haidt). Princeton University Press.
Wong, P. T. P. (Ed.). (2012). *The human quest for meaning: Theories, research, and applications* (2nd ed.). Taylor & Francis, Routledge.
World Health Organization. (1998). *WHOQOL-BREF*, Geneva.
Wrosch, C., Scheier, M. F., Miller, G. E., & Carver, C. S. (2012). When meaning is threatened: The importance of goal adjustment for psychological and physical health. In P. T. P. Wong (Ed.), *The human quest for meaning: Theories, research, and applications* (2nd ed., pp. 539–557). Taylor & Francis, Routledge.
Zhang, H., Sang, Z., Chan, D. K.-S., & Schlegel, R. (2019). Threats to belongingness and meaning in life: A test of the compensation among sources of meaning. *Motivation and Emotion, 43*, 242–254.

Index[1]

A
Acceptance, 26, 33, 40, 42, 57, 65, 68, 69
Ageism, 25
Agency, 11–13, 18, 19, 27, 41, 47, 48, 50, 59, 65
    See also Competence; Control
Age-period-cohort problem, 16
Aging, 5–7, 9–62, 64, 70, 73
Alma, Hans, 10, 11, 47
Antonucci, Toni C., 37
Apostel, Leo, 40
Arutyunova, Karina R., 21, 22
Atchley, Robert C., 39, 43

B
Bakewell, Sarah, 4
Balance, 12, 14, 40, 47–50, 53, 59, 69
Bauer, Jack J., 56, 57

Baumeister, Roy F., 10, 13, 20, 23, 24, 29, 31, 36, 47, 52–54, 53n19, 56, 58, 58n23
Biographical pain, 22, 28
Bohlmeijer, Ernst, 33
Boredom, 12, 32
    See also Excitement
Braam, Arjan, 17, 43

C
Care, 10, 40, 45, 47, 54, 65, 71
Career, 5, 29
Carstensen, Laura L., 15, 16, 43n12
Coherence, 10–12, 15, 27–31, 42–44, 52, 54, 57, 59
Colby, Anne, 18–20, 40n11, 53n20, 61, 62n24
Communion, 12, 41, 47, 48, 50, 65
    See also Connectedness

---

[1] Note: Page numbers followed by 'n' refer to notes.

© The Author(s), under exclusive license to Springer Nature Switzerland AG 2024
P. Derkx, A. B. Pinn, *Meaningful Aging from a Humanist Perspective*, https://doi.org/10.1007/978-3-031-53869-8

Compensation, 26, 47–50
Competence, 11, 65
    See also Agency; Control; Personal competencies
Completeness, 29
Connectedness, 11, 12, 17, 27, 36–44, 46–49, 54, 58n23, 59, 60, 65
    See also Communion
Continuity, 12, 30, 65
Control, 11, 12, 23, 25–28, 31, 39, 41–43, 46–49, 51, 52, 58–60, 69, 70, 75
    See also Agency; Competence
Copson, Andrew, 4
Côté, Stéphane, 22
Crescioni, A. Will, 20, 58n23
Crumbaugh, James C., 14
Culture, 13, 16, 21, 27, 32, 33, 46, 47, 59, 66
Curiosity, 12, 32
    See also Excitement; Wonder

D
De St. Aubin, Ed, 40, 41, 45, 46
Diener, Ed, 10, 44, 50, 51, 52n17
Divorce, 23, 38
Duyndam, Joachim, 2

E
Edmondson, Ricca, 10, 40, 46, 61, 62
Education, 4, 16, 26, 38, 42, 52, 73
Efficacy, *see* Control
Egloff, Boris, 25
Ego-integrity/ego integrity, 15, 28, 31, 40, 43, 57, 59
Enjoy(ment), 45, 71
Epstein, Greg, 5
Erikson, Erik H., 15, 17, 18, 28, 40, 41, 43, 45

Erol, Ruth Yasemin, 24
Excitement, 11, 12, 19, 31–35, 42, 43, 60, 65
    See also Curiosity; Wonder

F
Family, 19, 21, 34, 36, 48, 51, 55, 60
Farsides, Tom, 10, 11, 14, 31, 32, 50
Flourishing, 14, 52, 76
Frankl, Viktor, 9, 32
Freedom, 13, 19, 20, 35, 67, 67n1
Freeman, Mark, 30, 31
Friends, 23, 36–38, 48, 60
Fung, Helene, 16

G
Gecas, Viktor, 57
Gender, 19, 24, 64, 66, 70, 71, 73, 74, 76, 77
Generativity, 15, 17, 18, 40–43, 45, 46, 60
Gerotranscendence, 17, 40, 42, 43, 60
Goal, 3, 10, 11, 13–15, 18, 26, 28, 40, 41, 46, 49, 50, 59
    See also Purpose
Gorham, Candace, 5
Gruenewald, Tara L., 42

H
Happiness (happy life), 3, 4, 51–54, 53n19, 56–58, 65, 72
Health, 2, 2n1, 5, 14, 15, 18, 19, 25, 27n7, 33, 37–39, 37n10, 42, 52n18, 65, 75
Heine, Steven J., 59
Heintzelman, Samantha, 27, 28
Historical, 3, 4, 13, 26n6, 45–47, 60, 70, 75
Hortulanus, Roelof, 36–38

Hostile-world-scenario (HWS), 55, 56
Human agency, 13
Human dignity, 13, 68
Humanism, 4–7, 13, 14, 54, 64–72
Humanist, 2–7, 13, 14, 18n4, 22, 31, 64–69, 76
Human rights, 13

Life extension, 14, 64, 70–72, 76, 77
Life narrative (life story), 12, 28–30, 60
Loneliness, 14, 36–38, 37n10, 56, 58n23
Love, 13, 36, 38–40, 47, 68
Luciano, Eva C., 24

I
Identity, 12, 15, 28, 30, 48, 65, 66, 75
Interdisciplinary collaboration, 62
Interpretive control, 26
    See also Secondary control
Irving, Justine, 15, 16

J
Johnson, Malcolm, 22, 23, 28, 39
Jones, J. H., 72
Justice, 14, 64–77

K
Keyes, Corey L. M., 52, 52n18
King, Laura, 17, 27, 34, 56
Kohn, Melvin L., 46, 47n15
Kristjánsson, Kristján, 61
Kruse, Andreas, 28, 29, 40, 43

L
Laceulle, Hanne, 13, 14, 16–19, 22n5, 30, 31, 39, 53n20
Lamont, Corliss, 66
Learn, 45
Life course/life-course, 14, 16, 25, 26, 38, 41, 45, 51, 62
Life cycle, 15, 40, 45, 46
Life expectancy, 14, 17n3, 36

M
Machielse, Anja, 2, 36–38
Maholick, Leonard T., 14, 31n9
Marriage, 29, 30
Mastery, *see* Control
McAdams, Dan P., 12, 47, 56
McNair, Simon, 21
Meaning dimensions, 9–62
Meaning frame, 13, 64, 65, 68, 69
Meaning in life (meaningful life, meaningfulness), 3, 5, 7, 9–14, 17, 18n4, 23, 25, 27, 27n7, 30–32, 38, 39, 42, 44–60, 48n16, 64, 65, 71
Meaning needs, 14, 43, 58n23
Melton, Amanda, 32
Miyamoto, Yuri, 46, 47
Mooren, Jan Hein, 11, 27–29
Moral agency, 18, 19
Moral judgment, 18, 21, 22
Moral purpose, 18–20, 48
Moral worth, 10, 11, 17–23, 31, 36, 42, 47, 48, 52, 54, 57, 58, 60, 65
Morgan, Jessica, 10, 11, 14, 31, 32, 50

N
Narcissism, 24, 60
Narrative integration, 30, 31
Nietzsche, Friedrich, 10

O

Orth, Ulrich, 24, 25

P

Personal competencies, 38
Personal relationships, 12, 19, 36, 60
Piff, Paul K., 46
Popper, Karl R., 61
Pratt, Michael W., 17, 41, 42
Purpose, 10–12, 14–20, 23, 27, 28, 31, 31n9, 32, 35, 36, 42–44, 46–48, 51, 52, 53n20, 57, 59, 60, 62, 65, 76
See also Goal

Q

Quality of life, 10, 52, 64, 68, 71, 72, 75

R

Race, 6, 7, 64, 66, 71–74, 76
Religion, 5, 13, 14, 20, 21, 54
Retirement, 16, 18, 25, 26, 37n10, 38, 41, 60
Roberts, Alice, 4
Ryff, Carol D., 10, 14, 15, 31n9, 46, 47, 50–52, 52n17, 62n24

S

Schmitt, Eric, 28, 29, 40, 43
Schmukle, Stefan, 25
Schooler, Carmi, 46, 47n15
Schulenberg, Stefan, 32
Schwab, Joseph R., 56
Schwalbe, Michael L., 57
Schwartz, Shalom H., 20, 21, 48, 62
Secondary control, 26
See also Interpretive control

Selection, optimization, and compensation, 26
Self-acceptance, 11, 24, 51, 52
Self-esteem, 11, 23–25, 48n16, 57, 58
Self-realization, 13, 16, 18, 19, 53n20
Self-respect, 11, 23, 24, 38
Self-worth, 11, 12, 23–25, 31, 42, 43, 46–48, 52, 57–60, 58n23, 65
See also Self-esteem
Shmotkin, Dov, 39, 51, 52, 55–57, 56n21, 56n22
Shrira, Amit, 51, 55–57, 56n21, 56n22
Smaling, Adri, 10, 11, 47
Social network, 37, 38
Socioeconomic status (SES), 14, 24, 25, 46, 47
Socioemotional selectivity theory, 15, 16, 43n12
Sools, Anneke, 33
Specht, Jule, 25, 26
Spirituality, 20, 39–44
Stability, 2, 21, 30, 51, 52, 65
Stage (stage in life), 15, 40, 44
State (state of mind), 44
Sternberg, Robert, 36
Strategy (adaptive mechanism), 44, 55

T

Thomä, Dieter, 30
Tornstam, Lars, 17, 42, 43
Trait (personality trait), 42–44, 59, 60
Trent, Jason, 27
Tsai, Jeanne, 32, 33

V

Value, 3, 5, 7, 11–13, 18–21, 23, 30, 30n8, 32, 41, 43, 48, 52, 61, 62, 64–69, 73–76
van de Goor, Jacky, 33–35
van Praag, J.P., 27, 31

W
Walker, Margaret Urban, 39, 48
Washington, H. A., 72
Webster, Noah J., 37
Well-being, 2, 4, 5, 7, 10, 16, 18,
 25, 39–41, 44, 47, 50–57,
 52n17, 52n18, 59, 60,
 65, 68, 75
Westerhof, Gerben, 33
Widowhood, 25
Wonder, 33
 See also Curiosity; Excitement

Work, 2, 5, 6, 10, 13, 16, 19, 34, 38,
 45, 50, 61, 62, 64, 67, 70, 72–74
Worldview, 5, 6, 13, 14, 18n4, 22,
 28, 29, 64

Y
Yamada, Yoko, 45

Z
Zhang, Hong, 48–50, 48n16

Printed in the United States
by Baker & Taylor Publisher Services